Authentic Assessment:
Active, Engaging Product and Performance Measures

Sandra Schurr

Association for Middle Level Education
Westerville, Ohio

Library of Congress Cataloging-in-Publication Data

Schurr, Sandra.
Authentic assessment : active, engaging product and performance measures / Sandra Schurr.
   p. cm.
Includes bibliographical references.
ISBN 978-1-56090-245-4
1. Educational tests and measurements--Handbooks, manuals, etc. 2. Middle school students--Rating of--Handbooks, manuals, etc. 3. Active learning--Handbooks, manuals, etc. 4. Student-centered learning--Handbooks, manuals, etc. I. Title.
LB3051.S3392 2012
371.26--dc23
                2011042509

Association for Middle Level Education
formerly National Middle School Association
4151 Executive Parkway, Suite 300, Westerville, Ohio 43081
tel: 800.528.6672   fax: 614.895.4750   www.amle.org

AMLE™

About the Author

Sandra L. Schurr was the Director of the National Resource Center for Middle Grades/High School Education and Associate Professor in the College of Education at the University of South Florida from 1985 through 2010. A former classroom teacher, building principal, and school district administrator, Dr. Schurr, known internationally for her dynamic workshops and training programs, is the author of many AMLE publications that have been widely acclaimed by classroom teachers for their imaginative and practical instructional and assessment activities.

Appreciation is expressed to Carla Weiland of AMLE who was instrumental in making this book a research-based, readable document.

Contents

Preface

Since 1990 when I first wrote about authentic assessment, thanks to technology, the number of possible products and performances students can use or apply to demonstrate their learning has indeed mushroomed. However, the basic reasons for assessing authentically remain the same. It is developmentally appropriate and student-centered, it emphasizes life skills and abilities, it has the capacity to challenge students on differing levels of understanding, it engages students in their own progress and achievement, it empowers students, it acknowledges multiple learning styles, intelligences, aptitudes, and interests, and ultimately celebrates diversity.

This book, which is based on my 1999 book *Authentic Assessment from A to Z: Using Product, Performance, and Portfolio Measures,* aims to help middle grades educators align assessment measures (portfolio, product, performance options) with standards-based curriculum by providing active learning strategies that can be used formatively or summatively. The book provides nearly everything needed to understand and put into practice more informative and comprehensive assessments than can be delivered by standardized tests alone.

21st Century Skills

As Jill Spencer says in *Everyone's Invited: Interactive Strategies that Engage Young Adolescents:*

> Twenty-first century adults need the capacity to continue learning new information and skills and to be flexible and adaptive thinkers. Creativity and problem solving or what we used to call "Yankee ingenuity" (at least in my part of the world) will continue to be integral to a vibrant economy and culture. These skills and habits of mind will not burst forth fully formed from an 18-year-old's brain without incubation throughout his or her pre-K through 12 education experience. Since our students' problem-solving and reasoning skills are just emerging, we have an obligation to help them to learn to think critically. We want all of our students to be successful in college-prep and challenging career-prep courses so that they have true choices when they graduate from high school. Taking the time to provide concrete learning experiences that develop thinking patterns must be integral to our curriculum and instruction ... *Remember, we are trying to build lifelong learners* (p. 34).

Technology

In Differentiating Instruction with Technology in Middle School Classrooms, Grace Smith and Stephanie Throne make the case for technology as a bridge to high academic achievement through its use in relevant, meaningful, personalized learning. And research supports integrating technology into teaching and learning activities to help students achieve academically (ISTE, 2009). That said, don't panic. There are all sorts of ways to ease into the use of technology in authentic assessments—and students will lead the way once they are engaged in projects that have real meaning for them. They will find (or already know) the fastest, easiest way to gather information and perform tasks; your job will be to help them critically think about their information sources and to help them focus on the important questions. You probably won't know all the answers to whatever they decide to explore, but you do have the experience and skill to help them problem solve, look at issues from multiple perspectives, and challenge them to do their very best so they can be successful.

Book Organization

Part I, *Starting Points,* through a question-and-answer format, provides an explanation of what authentic assessment is and how it can be implemented. Following is a set of information sheets showing students the huge range of possible products and performances as well as research and Internet guidelines.

Part II, *Fifty Assessment Strategies,* sets forth detailed explanations of specific activities that can be used to authentically assess student progress. Both teachers and students need to become familiar with the many possibilities, some of which are fairly complex and involved. In this way, individuals or small groups will be able to decide on an appropriate strategy to direct their work and demonstrate their learning.

Part III, *Additional Resources,* provides a wealth of authentic assessment resources including sample rubrics and criteria to use in designing rubrics. Again, both students and teachers should become aware of this collection in order to recognize the available resources.

Part IV, *Teacher Study Materials,* provides two pieces of literature for teachers or teams to reflect upon, discuss, and clarify their thinking about. Guiding questions plus a glossary of assessment terms are also included as well as a bibliography of suggested resources for further study.

Part 1

Starting Points

I. FAQs About Authentic Assessment

1. What is authentic assessment?

Authentic assessment refers to measuring a student's abilities and/or achievements in relatively real-life contexts. "Real-life" may be understood from the vantage point of the student's everyday life or from the vantage point of adult expectations and the wider community. Authentic assessment efforts challenge the student with tasks that are potentially worthwhile, significant, and meaningful to both the student and others. These efforts may involve assessments of performances, products, portfolios, or attitudes and values.

Authentic assessment characteristically

- Involves an audience or the public.
- Is not constrained by arbitrary or unrealistic time limits.
- Has questions or tasks known up front.
- Requires collaboration with others.
- Merits worthwhile rehearsal and repetition.
- Employs higher-level critical and creative thinking skills.
- Is complex, open-ended, and draws on many capacities at once.
- Uses students' own research and background knowledge as a means not an end.
- Is attempted by all students and "scaffolded up" if necessary, rather than "dumbed down."

Authentic assessment is usually evaluated

- So that students can be aware of their own progress and achievement and as part of their learning.
- By performance (criterion-referenced) rather than by comparison to peers (norm-referenced).
- According to logical and reasonable criteria students understand.
- By self-assessment, wholly or in part.
- With a multifaceted scoring system rather than one aggregate grade.
- In ways that acknowledge multiple student learning styles, intelligences, aptitudes, and interests.

2. How does authentic assessment differ from traditional assessment?

Characteristics of Traditional Assessment	Characteristics of Authentic Assessment
1. Sequence of simple, distinct tasks	1. General, complex task involving interrelated sub-tasks
2. Recall of limited amounts of knowledge, despite ever-increasing scope of knowledge	2. Internalization and appreciation of knowledge and thinking processes generalizable to all sorts of knowledge
3. Quick and easy to score objectively, even if there is little validity	3. Scoring requires complex and more subjective considerations
4. Tests breadth of knowledge better (e.g., by numerous questions)	4. Tests depth of knowledge better
5. Easy to compare scores	5. Scores tend to be too contextual to compare easily
6. Easy to standardize for all students regardless of differences	6. Adapts more to unique strengths, needs, and choices of students
7. Encourages low-level thinking to arrive quickly at one right answer	7. Encourages critical and creative thinking, taking time to arrive at the best of many possible answers
8. Requires only reactive response, usually by student in isolation	8. Involves students very actively and cooperatively in productive process

Old Assessment Paradigm	New Assessment Paradigm
All students are basically the same and learn in the same way; therefore, instruction and testing can be standardized.	There are no standard students. Each is unique; therefore, instruction and testing must be individualized and varied.
Norm- or criterion-referenced standardized test scores are the main and most accurate indicators of student knowledge and learning.	Performance-based, direct assessment, involving a variety of testing instruments gives a more complete, accurate, and fair picture of student knowledge and learning.
Paper-and-pencil tests are the only valid way to assess academic progress.	Student-created and maintained portfolios, which include paper-and-pencil tests as well as other assessment tools, paint a more holistic picture of students' progress.

Assessment is separate from the curriculum and instruction; that is, there are special times, places, and methods for assessment.	The lines between the curriculum and assessment are blurred; that is, assessment is always occurring in and through the curriculum and daily instruction.
Outside testing instruments and agents provide the only true and objective picture of student knowledge and learning.	The human factor, that is, people subjectively involved with students (for example, teachers, parents, and the students themselves) holds the key to an accurate assessment process.
There is a clearly defined body of knowledge that students must master in school and be able to demonstrate or reproduce on a test.	Teaching students how to learn, how to think, and how to be intelligent in as many ways as possible (that is, creating lifelong learning) is the main goal of education.
If something can't be objectively tested in a uniform and standard way, it isn't worth teaching or learning.	The process of learning is as important as the content of the curriculum; not all learning can be objectively tested in a standardized manner.
The student is a passive learner, an empty receptacle to be filled.	The student is an active and responsible learner, and thus a partner with the teacher in the learning process.
Curriculum and school goals are to be driven by tests and test scores.	Curriculum and school goals are to be driven by a desire to tap the full intelligence and learning potential of students.
The bell curve, used to sort students into categories of successful, average, and failing (on a given test on a given day), is a reliable assessment of students' knowledge and abilities.	The J curve is a reliable assessment of students' knowledge and abilities, for it shows the growth of knowledge and abilities in a compounding fashion.
Monomodal testing practices (verbal-linguistic and logical-mathematical, that is, 'reading writing, and 'rithmetic') are the only viable means of testing students.	Multimodal testing practices based on the multiple intelligences (including visual-spatial, bodily-kinesthetic, musical-rhythmic, interpersonal, as well as verbal-linguistic, logical-mathematical, and naturalist) are all viable means of testing students.
Educators should use a behaviorist model to understand human development.	Educators should use a humanistic/developmental model to understand human development.
All students should be tested at the same time, using the same testing instruments, which are evaluated using the same criteria, giving educators a way to compare and contrast a student's achievement with that of other students.	Students are at varying developmental stages; testing must therefore be individualized and developmentally appropriate and should provide educators with information about how to read and teach them more effectively, producing students who are more successful more of the time.

The efficiency of an assessment approach (that is, easy to score, easy to quantify, easy to administer) is the paramount concern when developing tests.	The benefits to students' learning is the paramount concern when developing tests; efficiency is not an issue if assessment serves the needs of students and helps them improve their lives.
Assessment should be used to point out student failure, make comparisons among students, and rank students to determine their "standing" in the school.	Assessment should be used to enhance and celebrate student learning, to deepen understanding, and to expand students' ability to transfer learning to life beyond formal schooling.
Teaching and learning should be focused on curriculum content and acquiring data.	Teaching and learning should be brain compatible and focused on the learning process, the development of thinking skills, and understanding the dynamic relationships between curriculum content and real life.
Academic progress and success should be measured using traditional, predetermined, standardized criteria and instruments.	Academic progress should be measured using current, research-based educational practices that take into account individual needs, differences, and cognitive and psychological factors.
Learning is the mastery or understanding of various bits of objective, factual information such as dates, processes, formulas, figures, and so on.	Learning is first and foremost a subjective affair in which one's understanding of self and world is transformed, expanded, questioned, deepened, upset, stretched, and so on.
Successful teaching is preparing students to achieve on various tests designed to assess their knowledge in different subjects.	Successful teaching is preparing students for effective living throughout their lives; it therefore focuses on "teaching for transfer" of learning beyond the classroom, into one's daily living.

Source: Lazear, David (1994). *Multiple intelligence approaches to assessment: Solving the assessment conundrum.* Zephyr Press: Tucson, Arizona.

3. What are the differences among *alternative assessment, authentic assessment,* and *performance assessment*?

The terms are all used in discussions of assessment reform. Although these terms are sometimes used synonymously, they have different meanings. The term *alternative assessment* applies to any and all assessments that differ from multiple choice, timed, one-shot approaches that characterize most standardized and classroom assessments. The term *authentic assessment* conveys the idea that assessments should engage students in applying knowledge and skills in the same way they are used in the world outside of school. Authentic assessment also reflects good instructional practice, wherein teaching to the test is desirable. *Performance assessment* is a broad term encompassing many of the characteristics of both authentic assessment and alternative assessment (Mitchell 1992), as cited in Marzano, Pickering, & McTighe, 1993.

Source: Marzano, R., Pickering, D., & McTighe, J. (1993). *Assessing student outcomes: Performance assessment using the dimensions of learning model.* Alexandria, VA: Association for Supervision and Curriculum Development.

4. What is product assessment?

Product assessment directly checks students' understanding of and proficiency in a topic or subject by allowing them to generate or create a product to show what they know and what they can do, either alone or in cooperation with others.

5. Why is product assessment desirable?

Product assessment gives concrete evidence of student learning. Because it calls for students to apply knowledge and skills rather than simply recall knowledge, it is more likely to reveal student understanding. Product assessment is well-suited to assessing application of content-specific knowledge, integration of knowledge across subject areas, and lifelong learning competencies such as effective decision making, communication, and cooperation. Students are often allowed to use their creativity and knowledge base to go beyond what has been formally taught.

6. What are some advantages of product assessment for the student?

When students are given opportunities to produce authentic products, they become more engaged in and committed to their learning. Product assessment is motivating because projects are stimulating, relevant, give a focus to efforts, and are something that can represent the student before an audience. While standardized assessments strive for uniformity, product assessment presents students with opportunities to express their individuality. Product assessments are positive, because they highlight what a student *can do* while also revealing what they need to learn or where to improve.

7. What are some common types of products?

Essays, stories, poems, songs, novels, scrapbooks, newspapers, encyclopedia entries, advertisements, editorial letters, diaries, transparencies, pamphlets, picture dictionaries, bulletin boards, scrolls, magazines, collages, post cards, puzzles, collections, blueprints, plays, letters, surveys, sketches, plans, designs, charts, graphs, maps, costumes, diagrams, notebooks, study cards, flash cards, articles, books, compositions, investigative reports, interviews, research papers, laboratory reports, 2- and 3-dimensional models, experiments, exhibits, inventions, artwork, games, filmstrips, films, collections, dioramas, photographs, drawings, paintings, mobiles, displays, musical instruments, machines, gardens, videotapes, musical compositions, audiotapes, compact discs, software programs, multi-media webpages. See pages 20–21 for a list of products.

8. How should products be evaluated?

Topics, themes, or concepts are chosen which could best be measured by assessing student products. Not all topics, themes, or concepts lend themselves equally well to product assessment. Students should be able to choose from optional product formats, and these should be as authentic as possible.

Then students should develop a plan and a schedule for creating their product. Teachers can help to ensure the process is manageable and focused. Once decisions are made, students should know the timetable, what materials are available, and when and how much class time will be provided.

Criteria are developed and selected and then incorporated into a scoring rubric or rating scale with characteristics listed for each score or level, a task-specific guide, or a checklist. Students should know criteria up front so they can use them in guiding their progress, in assessing themselves and their product during the development process, and in assessing peers.

Final grades should reflect numerical ratings as well as comments, observations, and recommendations. The process of product development may be assessed, but emphasis should be on the end result, the product itself. Students should display and share their products with an audience. They should have an opportunity to explain the process behind their product development. Final products can be placed in portfolios as part of portfolio assessment. Later they can serve as models of excellence for future students.

9. What is performance assessment?

Performance assessment is an assessment of how well individuals can do something, as opposed to determining what they know about doing something. It requires students to create an answer or product that demonstrates desired knowledge or skills. Performance assessments have long been practiced to some extent, e.g., calling students to the chalkboard to perform mathematical calculations or solve grammatical problems, science lab experiments, gymnastic exercises, and athletic competitions.

10. Why is performance assessment a valuable evaluation tool?

Performance assessment reveals more about an individual's ability to put understanding into practice than a written test can. Performance assessment tasks that use realistic and interesting scenarios expose students to real-world applications of what they are learning. They evoke complex and high-level thinking, communicating, and analysis skills.

11. What are some advantages of performance assessment for students?

Performance assessment provides immediate feedback to students. The tasks used in performance assessment are closer to real-life, authentic applications of learning.

12. What are some types of performance assessment?

Performance assessment tasks should be broad enough to evoke complex thinking, yet narrow enough to enable measuring evidence of learning. The tasks should fit with important educational objectives to justify the time and effort they require on the part of students and teachers. Typical performance assessment tasks include: projects; science fair exhibits; competitions; live performances in front of an audience; demonstration of content principles using examples or props; demonstration of procedures or techniques; group and collaborative projects involving planning, research, discussion, and presentation; oral presentations; responses to interviews; constructed-response questions (fill-in-the-blank, short answers, sketching graphs, writing steps for a mathematical proof); open-ended essays; and lab experiments. See pages 18–19 for a list of performance tasks.

13. How should performance assessments be evaluated?

The purpose of assessment and its relation to educational goals should be clearly understood by teachers, administrators, parents, and policymakers. Performance assessment requires judges to decide what level of quality a performance has reached in relation to established criteria in rubrics, checklists, or similar assessment tools. See page 88 for a sample performance rubric; you may want to have students customize the rubrics for their specific performance tasks.

Sample performances can be chosen ahead of time as *benchmarks* or *anchors,* representing what are typical for a given level of performance. If comparability of assessment is desired, then all judges whose assessment will be compared need to practice and be trained to assess like performances similarly.

14. What is a portfolio?

A portfolio is a systematic, integrated, and meaningful collection of a student's day-to-day work showing that student's efforts, progress, or achievement in one or more subjects. A portfolio includes evidence of the student's critical self-reflection and participation in setting the focus of the portfolio, selecting the contents of the portfolio, and judging the portfolio's merit.

15. What types of work should be included in the portfolio?

A portfolio should contain authentic samples of a variety of the student's accomplishments in both cognitive and affective domains. A portfolio might contain: essays, reports, letters, creative writing pieces, poetry, problems and solutions, response logs, reviews, journal entries, interviews, illustrations, maps, photographs, comic strips, dioramas, collaborative works, workbook exercises and quizzes, attitude surveys, reading lists, book reviews, self-assessment checklists, and statements, teacher comments and checklists, peer reviews, parental observations and comments, and rough drafts and revisions.

16. How should the portfolio be organized?

The portfolio can be organized by topic or subject, date completed, author (e.g., student, teacher, parent, administrator), ongoing vs. finished work, medium in which it is created, or rank in quality. To assist in understanding the portfolio, the way it is organized should be clarified up front. The portfolio should reveal growth and development over time and emphasize the processes involved in accomplishing the end goals.

17. How should a portfolio be graded or evaluated?

First all stakeholders—students, teachers, parents, administrators, local and non-local government should collaborate to form criteria (just as they did to form educational objectives). Then these criteria and standards are fitted to a measuring scale or *rubric*. The assessment process follows authentic ideals to assess the students, allow students to empower and assess themselves, evaluate and develop the curriculum, and evaluate the efficacy of the instruction. One of the most common tools or measures of the portfolio is the *checklist*.

18. Who selects the pieces to be included in the portfolio?

Students need to have a voice in how they and their achievements will be represented relative to the established criteria. Teachers, parents, peers, and possibly school administrators may help students decide for themselves what pieces ought to be included in the portfolio.

19. What are limitations and/or disadvantages of authentic assessment?

Scoring of authentic assessments tends to be complex and time-consuming because of the numerous considerations the tester must take into account. Instructors need to be specially trained and must personally be present to make the assessment (unlike traditional assessment that can use machines or other people to grade score sheets). The results from an authentic assessment are difficult (though not impossible) to make consistent, quantifiable, objective, or standardized.

20. How does one get started on authentic assessment options?

- Practice authentic instruction.
- Set goals compatible with authentic assessment and the needs of instruction.
- Devise tasks that can be made appropriately authentic and that test understandings and skills for which authentic assessment is best suited.
- Test the authentic assessment tasks and experiment with them to improve them.

21. What are ways to provide students with authentic audiences for the sharing of their work?

- When students are presenting, invite parents, grandparents, the principal, the counselor, the secretary, the class next door, or the custodian for half an hour.
- Individual students could share with parents and grandparents math processes they have mastered by using digital cameras, white boards, or SmartBoards.
- Invite senior citizens, stay-at-home parents, and other community members who have free time during the school day and who would be pleased to give feedback to students.
- Invite the recipients of the real project—elementary students who are the audience for an original children's book; recipients of service learning projects (managers of local food banks, parks, homeless shelters; local government official); other middle school classes.
- Teachers can learn from each other or from students how to use VoiceThread, Animoto, Glogster, SlideShare, Xtranormal and all the safe sites for students to publish their writing.
- Posting work on safe sites on the Web allows students to share their ideas and conclusions and receive feedback from interested people across the globe. Posting student work that can be commented upon is a motivator for middle grades students to take the extra time to improve the quality of their work (Spencer, *Teaming Rocks*, 2010, p. 53).

22. What are some strategies for having students practice their presentations?

Teach the art of presentation and give students enough practice time to feel comfortable sharing what they have learned.

- Set aside a block of time each day for a week for students to prepare for presenting.
- Invite a drama teacher or other person with speaking experience to lead the class in some exercises focusing on speaking and making eye contact.
- Have someone address students about making quality visuals for presentations.
- Have students practice their presentation with a partner. Then partners can join with another pair, and they practice again. Groups join again so that students practice in front of a larger group. The teachers roam through the groups offering suggestions and encouragement.

23. What are some cautions when implementing authentic assessment in the classroom?

Authentic assessment should be a part of continuous learning, not just a measure conducted at the end of instruction, or at the beginning and end. Instruction should focus on the "big picture", so students can integrate pieces of knowledge as they learn them and relate previously learned ideas to new ones. Students should have a positive, optimistic attitude about assessment. They should recognize that learning is a process, and that improving one's self is an ongoing task.

Authentic assessment needs to preserve the measurement ideals of validity (measuring what it intends to measure), *reliability* (providing dependable and consistent measurements, e.g., of the same student with no intervening change in circumstances), and *fairness* (giving all students an equal opportunity to show they know and can do what has been taught, without regard to past performance or personal bias).

Authentic assessment should also have clear instructional goals—what students are to learn, understand, and do. These goals may include *declarative knowledge* such as facts, concepts, or principles; *procedural knowledge* such as skills, processes, or strategies; or *attitudes* such as values or habits of mind. The purposes of the assessment need to be clear, too—is it for improving quality of instruction? To provide indicators of how well a class or school is doing? To make comparisons between schools?

References

Marzano, R., Pickering, D., & McTighe, J. (1993). *Assessing student outcomes: Performance assessment using the dimensions of learning model.* Alexandria, VA: Association for Supervision and Curriculum Development.

Spencer, J. (2010). *Teaming rocks! Collaborating in powerful ways to ensure student success.* Westerville, OH: National Middle School Association.

2. Ideas for Students to Consider When Deciding What To Do

Read about …

Interview someone …

Hypothesize about …

Use a computer to …

Do a survey to find out …

Write a story, play, or poem …

Draw a picture …

Assemble a bibliography …

Experiment …

Write a letter to …

Interpret or translate …

Volunteer your services to …

Observe and compare …

Redesign or invent …

Take a field trip to …

Construct a model …

Propose a solution to …

Start a campaign …

Teach a lesson …

Organize a panel, debate, or court trial …

Find examples of …

Make recommendations …

Draw conclusions …

Propose …

Justify or criticize …

Test for …

Explain results …

Write directions …

Analyze contributions …

Make predictions …

Dramatize …

Use manipulatives to …

Demonstrate …

Act out or role play …

Investigate origins of …

Reflect on …

Improvise …

Make a poster about …

Make a timeline for …

Create an instructional manual with diagrams of …

Write TV story board, script, or commercial to …

Make up a memorial service honoring …

Prepare a "Who's Who" of …

Write your reactions to ...

Trace the growth or evolution of ...

Design a book cover, album cover,
or covers of sheet music ...

Write a column about ...

Make an illustrated encyclopedia
page of the ...

Design a handout to ...

Create a balance or ledger
sheet of reasons why ...

Read and compare copies of versions of ...

Write a proposal to improve ...

Compile a directory of ...

Describe an encounter between ...

Construct a replica of ...

Make a special edition of ...

Do a study of ...

Paint a picture or mural about ...

Write a headline and
accompanying article for ...

Write a picture book about ...

Draw a ladder showing the steps for ...

Illustrate or explain the words of ...

Make up a survival manual for ...

Design a community bulletin
board advertising ...

Write a case for or against ...

Create a series of slides or
photos to show ...

Compose a minute-by-minute
account of the day of ...

3. Research Checklist for Students

Directions. Use this simple checklist to record the varied resources, references, and methods which you have used to conduct your research on a given topic.

ABOUT MY RESEARCH

The topic I chose to research is: _____

I chose this topic because: _____

Check all the sources you used to answer your research questions and note whether the source is a primary or secondary source.

____ Library or reference books	____ DVDs or CDs
____ Internet websites	____ Interviews
____ Atlas, map, or globe	____ Museum
____ Newspapers or magazines	____ Field visits
____ Encyclopedias	____ Agencies or organizations

____ Other, list: _____

____ I took notes on my research.

____ I recorded the resource/source information using APA style.

____ I organized the information into categories.

____ I synthesized the data collected and presented it in a "meaningful' whole.

____ I made appropriate generalizations and interpretations of the information gathered.

____ I was able to express the ideas from the research in my own words.

____ I wrote a first draft of the report.

____ I revised my first draft.

____ I had a friend or teacher read and react to my revised first draft.

____ I wrote and edited my final draft.

____ My research is ready to share and publish.

4. Locating Information from Common and Not-So-Common Sources

Visit

Museum

Shopping Center

Courtroom

Art Show or Institute

Laboratory

Stores and Businesses

Libraries

Agencies and Organizations

Internet websites

Tourist Attractions

Read

Books

Blogs

Brochures or Pamphlets

Warranties

Wikis

Magazines

Reports

Documents

Reviews and Critiques

Almanacs

Cartoons and Comic Strips

Newspapers

Journals

Listen

CDs or MP3s

Radio or Television Talk Shows

Conversations

Panels or Debates

Speeches

Presentations

Watch

DVDs

Movies

Slides

Television

Nature in Action

People in Action

Attend

Conferences

Seminars

Musical Performances

Plays or Musicals

Art Shows

Poetry Readings

Demonstrations

Classes

Webinars

Examine

Maps

Models

Charts

Tables

Graphs

Diagrams

Collections

Photographs

Documents

Flow Charts

Story Boards

CD and DVD Covers

Book Covers

Yellow Pages

Advertisements

Catalogs

Cookbooks

Dictionaries

Internet websites

Posters and Wall Charts

Schedules and Time Tables

Experience

Group Discussions

Role Playing

Field Experiences

Educational and Mind Games

People Watching

Cultural Events

Contests and Competition

Skype Calls

Podcasts

Learning a New Language

Travel

Interview

Service Learning

Training a Pet

Courtroom

Webinar

Working on a Political Campaign

5. Planning Outline for a Product or Performance Project

1. Write the major goal or purpose of your product or performance. List no more than three subgoals (smaller goals) to achieve in the project or performance. (For example: My major goal is to learn what parks are available in my community. My three subgoals are to find out (1) how they are spread out over the community, (2) if there are areas accessible to urban children, and (3) how much it costs to keep these areas open and accessible.)

2. Rewrite the goal or purpose and the objectives in the form of questions. (For example, what natural resources are available in my community? How are they spread out in the community? Are there areas accessible to urban children? How much does it cost to keep these areas open and accessible?)

3. List multiple sources of information you will use in researching your project. Consider use of Internet, audio visuals, reference books, encyclopedias, interviews, prints, DVDs, atlases, almanacs, maps, observations, field trips, and public records.

4. When using the Internet, evaluate sites using the guidelines on page 22, How to Evaluate a Web Source. Google is a search engine that you probably know how to use. Other search engines present sites in more visual ways, and you might try them as well.

    1. *http://search-cube.com* uses a visual cube that you can work with.

    2. *http://search.yippy.com* organizes the search results into categories.

    3. *http://bing.com* helps you narrow your search.

5. Describe the steps you will use to achieve all your goals and objectives. Write them in the order the steps will occur.

6. List at least three different methods that you can and/or will use to present your final project or performance.

7. Organize the project or performance into a detailed timeline using day and week intervals.

8. Briefly describe how you will edit, rehearse, and/or prepare for the delivery of the project or performance.

9. Determine how you will assess the quality and success of your project or performance. What feedback will be given? Who will provide the feedback? Who will analyze the feedback? Who will evaluate the feedback?

6. Types and Descriptions of Performance Tasks

Type of Task	Description
Definition	Define specific terms and concepts using dictionary-type diction with brief words of explanation or clarification as needed.
Memorization	Recall and recite a piece of information in its exact words and/or form.
Classification	Put into categories or groups certain people, places, or things.
Comparison and Contrast	State both similarities and differences of two or more people, places, or things.
Demonstration	Show or perform a specific skill or act.
Inference	Look for and identify between-the-lines meanings.
Prediction	Make realistic guesses about what could have happened or will happen in the future.
Application	Use knowledge or skill in a context or situation different from the one in which it was learned.
Construction	Build or develop a model, theory, or idea from scratch.
Experimentation	Experiment to test a hypothesis.
Generalization	Draw conclusions from a given set of data.

Investigation	Follow a reasonable set of guidelines for conducting an inquisition of or forming generalizations about an assigned topic or problem.
Analysis	Break down a whole into its component parts, looking for relationships between parts or the recognition of the organizational principles involved.
Analyzing Perspectives	Consider two or more different perspectives and then choose a perspective to support.
Invention	Create, compose, design, develop, or produce something new and unique.
Appraisal	Determine the worth or value of a person, place, thing, or idea.
Decision-Making	Identify the factors or variables that caused a certain decision to be made.
Problem-Solving	Create a solution to a specific problem.
Evaluation	Identify the pros and cons or advantages and disadvantages of a given situation.

7. Types of Product Formats

A is for … advertisement, albums, almanacs, anagram, anecdote, annotated bibliography, artifact collection, audio tape recording, autobiography, award

B is for … ballad, banner, bar chart, biography, blog, blueprint, book jacket, book report, booklet, bookmark, brochure, bullet chart, bulletin board, business letter

C is for … Calendar, campaign speech, cardboard relief, cartoon, CD, celebrity profile, characterization, charade, chart, checklist, choral reading/speech, cinquain, classification list, classified advertisement, collage, collection, column chart, comedy act, comic book, commercial script, computer program, conference presentation, costume, couplet, creative writing, critique, crossword puzzle

D is for … dance, database, debate, demonstration, description, design, device, diagram, dialogue, diary, dictionary, digital story, diorama, discussion, display, display case, documentary, dramatization, drawing, DVD

E is for … editorial, editorial cartoon, essay, etching, experiment, explanation

F is for … fact file, fairy tale, field manual, field trip, film, flag, flannel board, flash card, flip camera, flip chart, flowchart, free verse, friendly letter

G is for … gadget, gallery, game, glossary, graph, graphic, greeting card, guidebook

H is for … handbook, handout, hieroglyphic

I is for … icon, identification cards, identification chart, illustration, imprint, information table, instruments, interpretive dance, interview script, invention

J is for … jigsaw puzzle, jingle, job description, joke, joke book, journal, journal article

K is for … kite, king-size book cover or front page

L is for ... label, layout, learning center, lecture, lesson plan, letter, letter to edit, limerick, line chart, list, lithograph, log, lyrics

M is for ... magazine, magazine article, manual, map, mask, memorandum, mine, mobile, mock interview, model, monologue, monument, mosaic, movement game, movie, mural, museum, musical instrument, myth

N is for ... newscast, newsletter, newspaper, newspaper ad, newspaper article, notes, novel, nursery rhyme

O is for ... observation sheet, observations, oral report, origami, outline

P is for ... painting, pamphlet, papier mache, parody, pattern, pen pal, pennant, PERT Chart, petition, photo essay, photograph, pictograph, picture dictionary, pie chart, plan, play, poem, poster, prediction, profile, puppet show, puzzle

Q is for ... quatrain, questionnaire, quilt, quiz

R is for ... radio announcement, radio commentary, radio commercial, radio script, rap, recipe, recorded dialog, research report, review, rhyme, riddle, role-play

S is for ... satire, scatter graph, scenario, science fiction, scrapbook, scroll, short story, sign, silk, screen, skit, slide show, slogan, song, speech, stencil, story, story problems, storytelling, survey, symposium discussion

T is for ... tall tale, telegram, television commercial, television script, term paper, test, textbook, theory, timeline, transparency, travel advertisement, travel log, triplet

V is for ... video tape, vocabulary list, virtual experience

W is for ... wall hanging, weather map, web, word search, word wall, worksheet

Y is for ... yearbook

8. How To Evaluate a Web Source

Here are six ways to check the information on websites.

1. **Author:**
   Is it clear who has written the information?
   Is the person an authority on the topic?
   What are their credentials?

2. **Purpose:**
   Are the aims of the site clear?
   Why did the author publish this site?
   Does the site achieve its aims?

3. **Audience:**
   Is the site relevant to you?
   Does it fit the goal of your project?

4. **Accuracy:**
   Can the information be checked?
   What clues about the quality of information do the page
   construction, spelling, grammar, and the url give you?

5. **Publication:**
   When was the site produced?
   Is the information current?

6. **Viewpoint:**
   Is the information biased in any way?
   Is it clear what is fact and what is opinion?

Sources:"QUICK: The Quality Information Checklist" at http://www.avon.k12.ct.us/enrichment/Enrich/quickgrd4-0.htm and "Website Evaluation Form" at http://interactives.mped.org/view_interactive.aspx?id=177&title=

Fifty Authentic Assessment Strategies

Storyboard

Description

Storyboards are useful tools to help organize a story, newscast, play, sketch, or show you will write and/or any performance you will do. A storyboard can also be used as a visual aid for a display, an oral talk, or a group activity. Storyboards organize the writing or performance scene-by-scene using boxes. You can use the model on the next page to create your own storyboard.

Planning

1. Decide on a topic for the storyboard. Storyboards are useful for creating book reports, flipbooks, brochures, cartoons, videos, or presentations.

2. Outline the essential details of setting, characters, events, issues, problems, and solutions or conclusions essential to the proper telling of the story.

3. On a large piece of paper create a series of boxes to represent what happens to the relevant items from number two above as the story unfolds (see examples on next page). The size of the boxes should vary depending upon the type of information to be recorded. Adjust the boxes as necessary to make your plan for telling your story or planning your show.

4. If the storyboard is for

   a. a book report, you may want to make several storyboards. For example, there might be several character boxes (one for each major person) showing their development as the story progresses, several event boxes (one for each action that makes up the plot structure), several problem boxes (one for each different perspective represented), several solution boxes (one for each possible alternative), or several conclusion/solution boxes (one for each decision made).

   b. an interview for a talk show, you might want to group the questions in boxes according to various subjects you want to make sure that you cover.

   c. a demonstration that will be recorded digitally, you could plot out the sequence of events that will be occurring and designate when the materials should be filmed, when the speaker should be filmed, when the audience should be filmed, etc.

5. Use your storyboard to write your work; if you are doing a performance, rehearse your script until you are comfortable and remember easily what you are to do.

Assessing

1. What part of the storyboard did you visualize (see in your mind) most clearly?

2. What problem-solving or decision-making ideas were most difficult to summarize or portray in your storyboard? Why do you think this was the case?

3. Were there any loose ends or poorly described incidents in this story map that did not satisfy you or others? Describe them. How could you fix this?

4. What is the most important part of your storyboard? Why?

5. Would this storyboard make a good play, movie, video, or television show? Why or why not?

Technology Connection

1. If you have access to a digital video camera, have your teacher or a teammate record the performance of your work. Review the video on the digital camera or the computer after the performance and reflect on your work. You may need to view it several times to evaluate your voice quality, actions, and total effectiveness. Decide if you want to edit the film as is or do the performance again and re-record it. Once you are satisfied with the performance, you may want to add a title and other features, and save it on a computer.

2. For an online storyboard, check out *http://fcit.usf.edu/lmm/pdfs/Storyboards.pdf* or *http://www.the-flying-animator.com/storyboard-template.html*

Storyboard

Introduction:	Scene 1:	Scene 2:
Welcome to the show. Introduce topic of global warming and guests	Discuss general background about the global warming issue.	Experts talk about the effects of global warming; ask for sources backing up their opinions.
Scene 3:	Scene 4:	Scene 5:
Experts debate the issue of global warming	Experts answer questions from the audience.	The host summarizes the issue and concludes the show.

Create a Country or Culture

Description

Although every country or culture is unique, they share common features as well. One way of learning about the similarities and differences between different countries and cultures is to create an imaginary place and figure out how people develop, change, grow, and interact in this culture.

Planning

1. After deciding to invent a country or culture, the first step is to decide on a name for it. The name can come from a special historical place or period, from a particular belief system or philosophy, or from an important person or event. It is also important to determine the origin of the country or culture in terms of historical periods such as Ice Age, Industrial Revolution, Middle Ages, Neolithic Age, Twentieth Century, Renaissance, Bronze Age, Victorian Age, Colonization Age, or Space Age.

2. The second step in the process is to determine both geographical features of the area and the demographics of the people inhabiting it. Identify and describe such things as the natural resources, climate, landscape features, population size, growth rate, physical characteristics of the people, and their typical aging patterns, income levels, family size, and educational levels.

3. Then explain the most common structures for living quarters and buildings as well as the basic blueprint for city spaces vs. rural spaces. Communicate this information through maps, diagrams, sketches, drawings, or descriptions.

4. The next task is to plan the governmental, economic, and currency structures of the country or culture. Is it an aristocracy, democracy, monarchy, oligarchy, plutocracy, theocracy, dictatorship, or totalitarian type of government? Who leads the country or culture? What does the money look like? What denominations are there? What types of goods, services, and businesses dominate the economy?

5. Next, make decisions related to education, religion, rituals, and celebrations. How do people acquire educations and receive religious training? What rituals or rites of passage are key to the country or culture's continuation and growth? What holidays or celebrations are central to the beliefs and philosophy of the country or culture?

6. Finally, other aspects of the country or culture to consider in this project are:

    a. design of the clothing

    b. design of the flag

    c. creation of the anthem

d.　description of the toys, games, or sports

　　　e.　description of the common food, meals, or dishes

　　　f.　description of the dances, music, or drama

　　　g.　methods of defense or protection

7.　In a detailed paragraph, describe why people would want to visit your country or culture. Create a travel poster advertising the key elements of your proposed country or culture. Create a guidebook for tourists.

Assessing

1.　Using a scale of 0 (lowest number of points) to 10 (highest number of points), rate yourself on components of the project such as these.

　　　a.　The name and origin were carefully selected and documented according to a predetermined historical period.

　　　b.　The geographical features were consistent with its location.

　　　c.　Where people lived made sense in relation to other elements.

　　　d.　Living conditions, housing, and development of towns or cities were well-designed.

　　　e.　Descriptions and graphics of the government, economic, and currency structures were detailed and reasonable.

　　　f.　Education, religion, rituals, and celebrations were adequately depicted.

　　　g.　Other designated dimensions of the country were included in the overall creation of the place.

2.　Complete each of the starter statements below.

　　　a.　The strengths of this finished project are …

　　　b.　The parts of this finished project that could be improved are …

　　　c.　The most difficult part of this project for me was …

　　　d.　The easiest part of this project for me was …

　　　e.　The most enjoyable part of this project for me was …

　　　f.　Something I would do differently if I were to do a similar project would be …

Technology Connection

Using the Internet, collaborate with students in another country to create a country or culture. Work with the students to create a country that is "inviting, safe, and supportive of all." Share your ideas, writing, artwork, and music by using Skype and wikis; your teacher can search for students to partner with through epals or iEARN (the International Education and Resource Network).

Brochure

Description

A brochure is a popular format for advertising places or events, for sharing product or service information, for promoting tourist attractions, for offering special invitations, or for describing exciting exhibits and displays. Most brochures are two-sided, paper tri-folds that contain colorful illustrations, descriptions, charts, graphs, maps, or diagrams designed to provide the details needed to understand the subject of the brochure.

Examples of brochure topics are an imaginary trip to a rain forest or a national park, a local science museum, an outdoor garden, a medieval castle, an Egyptian pyramid, a pioneer village, or a southern plantation. Product brochure examples include books or inventions, and performance brochures could invite audiences to plays, skits, or concerts.

Planning

1. Visit a travel agent, a motel/hotel lobby, a tourist information center, or an American Automobile Association (AAA) agency to pick up several different brochures about events or attractions in your community.

2. Study these brochures and list all the different things they promote and the types of information they present. Note their diverse layouts and how effective the layouts are in presenting information.

    a. Rank order the brochures you collected at the start of the project from your least favorite to your most favorite. Determine what characteristics distinguish your favorites from your least favorites.

    b. Using these findings, establish a set of criteria for judging the appeal and accuracy of your finished brochure. Organize your criteria into a rubric format.

3. Next, decide on a specific part of the topic you have studied that would be suitable for making a brochure.

4. Decide the information to be printed in the brochure and research all areas to be discussed, described, or illustrated. The brochure's purpose is to accurately depict a location, subject, or performance so that the reader will be interested in visiting or learning more about it. Be sure to include graphics and illustrations to highlight special features.

5. Fold a legal size paper (8½" x 14") into thirds. Try to organize the information to be shared so that each of the six sections of the brochure has a specific purpose or focus. Try to vary the types of graphics, the size of typeface, the location of charts/diagrams/graphics, the length of copy, and the placement of titles.

Assessing

1. After filling out a rubric to evaluate your work, ask your teacher and your teammates to evaluate your brochure using the rubric you developed.

2. Collect the rubrics and compare them. What parts of the brochure captured what you wanted to convey about your topic? What would you do differently next time to improve the quality of your brochure?

Technology Connection

1. Storyboard your brochure at *http://fcit.usf.edu/lmm/pdfs/Storyboards.pdf*

2. "Use Word to Create a Tri-Fold Brochure" by Susan Daffron at: *http://www.computorcompanion.com/LPMArticle.asp?ID=143*

3. "Create a trifold brochure" at *www.studio.adobe.com*

One-Person Show

Description

In a one-person show, you assume the identity of a book character, a historical figure, a famous scientist, or an artist at work—and you stay in character throughout the performance and through its conclusion. This sort of performance allows you to show how your research or project "fits" into the world—how your theme or topic relates to the world in terms of people, places, culture, and time period. Taking on the persona of a historical person allows you to have some fun interacting with your audience as you stay in character while talking with them about their modern lives. Not only will you be demonstrating how much you have learned about your person, you will be practicing your oral presentation or acting skills and your thinking-on-your-feet skills.

Planning

1. Decide who you will be—you need not be a famous person; you can take on the role of a "regular" person in any time period or line of work, as long as you can relate the person to the topic of your research.

2. Figure out what the central message is that you want your character to give the audience. Are you teaching about a person's life and how he or she was influenced to make a discovery? Are you sharing what it was like to be a member of the upper class in a different time period? Are you showing how hard it was to exist without modern conveniences?

    a. What is the central moment your show will focus on? What changed your world? What happened after this moment?

    b. What are the important moments that led up to the central moment? What was happening in your life?

    c. Did the central moment change you?

    d. What people did you spend time with? What was your family like? How did you spend your free time? What kinds of thoughts ran through your head?

3. Other decisions to make:

    a. What will you wear?

    b. What props will you need?

    c. What words will you speak or actions will you demonstrate?

    d. What message will you give?

    e. What will you tell the audience about the life of your character?

4. List some questions that your character might ask the audience members during the show.

5. Outline or storyboard your performance.

6. Practice your performance (in costume) and get feedback from someone you trust.

7. Read the Rubric for Performance Assessment so that you know how your performance will be evaluated.

8. Gather all the materials and props you'll need, and first practice your part alone and then with a person you trust as your audience. Make sure your audience asks you questions and don't hesitate to engage him or her in conversation.

9. When you are ready, ask your teacher to schedule class time for your show.

Assessing

1. Ask your audience members and teacher to fill out a Rubric for Performance Assessment. Fill one out yourself.

2. Based on the rubric results, do you think your audience enjoyed your performance? Do you think they learned the information and concepts you wanted to convey?

3. What were the things you did best? What things do you want to learn how to do better the next time?

Technology Connection

1. Create a podcast (*www.commoncraft.com/show*) by recording and/or filming your show.

2. Share with others through VoiceThread (*http://voicethread.com*).

3. Make a 30-second ad for your show at this site for easy, free video production: *http://www.animoto.com*

5

Cartoon

Description

Cartoons can be an excellent means for explaining concepts and content, expressing opinions and feelings, summarizing ideas and theories, and enhancing reports and projects. They provide a way to convey important thoughts using both words and pictures.

Cartoons and comic strips have advantages over other forms of reporting. They are short with a few well-chosen words, and the simple drawings can be creatively and cleverly designed.

Before you do a cartoon report, become familiar with the art and science of cartooning. Try these warm-up exercises:

1. Study the comic section of your newspaper and note the size of the frames.

2. Study comic books and note how cartoonists use exaggerations in the drawings of the figures; how they use balloons and bubbles to show what cartoon characters are saying, doing, or thinking; how they draw faces to show varied expressions; and how the size of letters shows various pitches and intensity of voices and sounds.

3. Study a selection of editorial cartoons (cartoons on the editorial pages; usually political or social in nature) from newspapers and magazines to determine how these cartoons express opinions, make important points, and offer personal comments on current events mostly through the use of exaggeration and insults.

Planning

1. Collect and cut out a wide variety of cartoons and comic strips that appeal to you. Paste them into a mini-scrapbook or on a large poster and write characteristics you see in these examples that you could use in your own cartooning. Try to summarize the major idea, message, or episode that is being conveyed by the cartoonist.

2. Decide on a topic for your cartooning project. There are suitable topics in all subject areas. You can use cartooning to design a display or billboard, retell a fable or myth, and/or explain the meaning of vocabulary words or parts of speech. Cartooning can also highlight the accomplishments of a famous explorer, the action of a famous leader, or the life of a pioneer. It can illustrate the life cycle of a frog, the formation of rocks, or the habitats of endangered species. And cartoons can even explain math processes, geometric formulas, and how to solve word problems.

3. Determine the major concepts, terms, theories, or events you want to show in your cartoon. This preplanning will help you decide on the total number of frames you will need as well as what will go in each one. Make one or two rough drafts.

4. Construct your cartoon or comic strip on heavy drawing paper using fine-tipped magic markers or colored pens and pencils. Refer to your scrapbook samples for ideas on development of cartoon characters and dialogue. Be sure that each frame of the comic strip shares important information on the topic so that the reader can learn something from it.

Assessing

1. Count the number of cartooning features that you were able to incorporate into your own cartoon/comic strip project.

2. Count the number of major ideas and terms that you were able to incorporate.

3. Evaluate how well you were able to use cartooning as a means for reporting the information you had researched by adding the totals from numbers one and two above and by judging the quality of information on the topic that you taught. Ask readers of your comic strip to help you assess your work by telling you everything they learned about the topic from your cartoon.

Technology Connection

The Comic Creator at *www.readwritethink.org/files/resources/interactives/comic* allows you to compose dialogue and to choose backgrounds, characters, and props for cartoons.

6

Sketch Journal

Description

A sketch journal is like a journal kept by explorers on an expedition, an anthropologist at a dig in the field, or a sculptor in the studio. It involves the daily practice of making observations and then sketching those observations and writing short entries of personal comments, reflections, notes, and explanations. For example, a sketch journal about a real or virtual trip to Alaska might include an outline map of the area visited, short news clippings about events reported in the local paper, notes on salmon spawning, sketches of local wildlife, visual impressions of Glacier Bay, diagrams of boats and seaplanes traveled on, and sketches of tourist attractions, shops, or restaurants visited. In short, a sketch journal is a record of impressions and visuals on a given topic.

Planning

1. A good way to get started with a sketch journal is to begin each day by drawing a simple figure or sketch or by writing a "daily note," which involves nothing more than reflecting on what you, as a student, have learned or experienced in school the previous day. This will give you practice before you make a sketch journal based on your research.

2. Select a topic to explore through the development of a sketch journal. This is a good format to use for reporting on people, places, things, or events. Sketch journals are good sources of information on everything from famous battles in the Revolutionary War to a space landing on the moon.

3. After selecting your topic, make a list of possible entries for the sketch journal that can include such visuals as diagrams, maps, charts, graphs, blueprints, drawings, simplified notes, symbols, rebus stories, cartoons, stick figures, or even questions.

4. Research the topic and make daily entries in your sketch journal about the information you have learned. Use as many visuals and graphics as possible, and make notations to tie the journal entries together.

Assessing

1. Review the number of visuals recorded in your sketch journal. Determine what important data or information each represents. Then, decide whether each visual is as effective or efficient as a narrative description might have been in its place.

2. Judge which visual (or visuals) best conveys a major idea of your topic.

3. Write a paragraph pointing out the advantages and disadvantages of a sketch journal for reporting research information over a journal with narrative entries.

Wall Chart

Description

Sometimes it is easier to explain things with pictures and labels than with words and paragraphs. A wall chart is a labeled picture, diagram, or figure that displays information on a topic. Wall charts share basic information in a creative layout of artwork, brief captions, headings, small blocks of information, and borders or frames. Wall charts can be prepared using many different media such as crayons, colored pencils, magic markers, paint, cutout letters, collage, or combinations of these options. Wall charts created in a series can depict a given subject or theme with each wall chart covering a subtopic within that overall theme.

Planning

1. The key to a good wall chart is selecting an appropriate topic that lends itself to explanations with pictures, labels, and mini-texts rather than long paragraphs. Therefore, take time to choose a suitable topic, and as you research the information needed, think of ways to visually present the major concepts.

2. Next, sort out the information you want to portray and decide how best to present it. Sketch a layout for the chart and figure out on which sections of the chart you can place diagrams, figures, or pictures and on which sections you can place blocks of information. Consider where on the chart you will need connecting arrows or lines. Use this visual outline as a basis for writing your wall chart report. Sketch the artwork and compose labels and headings that will help to tell the story.

3. Consider using brief but large headlines as titles for major sections and smaller subheadings as points of clarification. Under the subheadings, write small blocks of text that contain important facts to make the topic of your wall chart more informative.

4. The layout and organization of the chart is important and should use arrows and lines to show how parts of the chart connect or relate.

5. Finally, make certain to put something eye-catching at the top of the chart to attract people's attention. Borders and frames can also add special interest and highlight major pieces of the text.

Assessing

1. For each of the following, assign point values on this scale: Outstanding 5; Excellent, 4; Good 3; Fair 2; Unsatisfactory 1: labeled illustrations, diagrams, and/ or figures; labels or headings; smaller subheadings, small blocks of information; interesting layout; connecting arrows and/or lines; title, heading, box at top; border or frame; varied print or font sizes, but not too many; engages other students; has eye appeal and tells story with visuals and words.

2. Add up the points and translate the total into a letter grade; explain your results.

"No-Sew" Quilt

Description

Historically, quilts were created to tell a story, share a culture, offer a visual representation of an event, or depict a series of scenarios around a common theme. There are many advantages of making a quilt project that doesn't involve sewing cloth squares. The pieces of the quilt and the quilt itself can be of varying sizes, they can include both pictures and words to tell a story or report a message, they are easy to construct, and they are interesting to interpret. You can adapt a quilt format to any subject area and to any combination of stories and information about people, places, things, or events.

Planning

1. Decide on a topic or theme for the quilt. Subjects can range from historical events or geographical sites to the recording of biographical data or important discoveries. Science quilts can show species, biomes, geological features, or physics principles.

2. Research the topic and write a set of important facts about the main ideas related to the topic. Decide how many pieces or squares you will include in your quilt project and then list the facts and corresponding graphics you will want to include on each piece. The quilt can include a graphic and a set of facts for each piece, or it can alternate a graphic with its corresponding set of facts. Either format works well.

3. Cut out several different-sized pieces for your quilt, and use these to determine the best size for your project. Consider whether you will have separate illustrated and factual sections or whether you will combine the two elements. Next, cut out several pieces for your quilt and number them. Write out a concept and/or a type of graphic to be used for each piece so that the pieces actually become a working outline for your research.

4. Draw each scenario and/or write each set of facts on the paper squares. Use a construction paper border around the outside of the quilt and between the individual pieces to hold the quilt together. Another option would be to paste the individual quilt pieces on a roll of shelf paper so that the finished quilt design is horizontal and a rectangle rather than a large square.

5. Practice retelling the story or reporting information using the squares or sections of the quilt.

Assessing

1. Determine whether the topic you have chosen is effectively shown in the quilt. Does the number of pieces get the information across? Is the quality of information good? What about the color and the pictures included? Is the shape and configuration a match for the subject? Does it have good eye appeal? Summarize your thoughts in a paragraph that critiques your finished product.

2. Share your quilt project with three other people and ask each one to critique your work. How do their comments compare with your analysis of your quilt? What things do you agree on, and what things do you disagree on? What would you do differently next time?

Critique

Description

Critiques identify and analyze the pros and cons of a product or service to determine whether it is of desired quality or not. They can also help you determine if a product is a good value by comparing its features or benefits to similar products in the same price range. Critiques can be developed on a wide range of products, including books, movies, theater productions, music albums, restaurants, cars, computers, vacation resorts, and amusement parks. If your parents bought you a laptop for school, they probably read lots of critiques or reviews prior to making the purchase to make sure it would do everything you needed it to do at the best price possible.

Planning

1. Look up online reviews of something you are genuinely curious about. For instance, if there is a new music group you have been hearing about, and you want to find out what critics are saying about their debut album, do an online search for reviews/critiques of the album. Find at least two reviews of the same product. Print the reviews and then compare them to see if they agree, or if they contradict each other.

2. In each instance, try to put yourself in the shoes of the reviewer/critic. What kinds of questions do you think the critic would have asked himself/herself before writing the critique? How did this person go about forming an opinion about the product? Write down at least three questions you think this person would have asked himself/herself about the product.

3. Choose a product that you have in your possession and are familiar with (book, music album, movie, laptop, MP3 player, etc.) to review. What do you think are the three most important questions to ask yourself about the product? What would make this a quality product? Write these questions, leaving plenty of space to answer them. First give a simple answer to each question, then give reasons for each simple answer.

4. Go back to the reviews you printed from the Internet and study how the critics organized their thoughts into coherent reviews for readers. Try to organize your answers and reasons in a similar fashion. Now write a review of your product that you think would help readers decide whether or not to purchase the product. When you have a clean draft of your full review typed, have at least one other student read the review and give you feedback about what would make it a stronger review. Take this feedback into consideration when preparing your final review. Your teacher may decide to post the reviews on the class or school website to help other students in making purchasing decisions.

Assessing

1. Carefully analyze your review. If you were thinking about purchasing this particular product, would you find your review helpful in making a decision?

2. Get feedback from several other students to see if they feel your review would help them in making a purchasing decision.

3. What do you think you did well in your review? What do you think you could have done better or in addition to make your review even better? If you are not sure, ask others for input.

4. Now that you have written your own review, will you be more likely to read reviews of products prior to making future purchases? What information will you be looking for in the reviews?

Technology Connections

Here is a list of websites you might find helpful in your search for examples of reviews.

Books

http://www.teenreads.com/reviews/index.asp
Professional reviews of young adult literature

Sites where students can post their book reviews:
http://www.readwritethink.org/classroom-resources/lesson-plans/thumbs-students-writing-publishing-976.html
http://www.worldreading.org
http://www.spaghettibookclub.org
http://www.buildingrainbows.com

Cars

http://www.edmunds.com/car-reviews/car-reviews-road-tests.html

Movies

http://rogerebert.suntimes.com
http://www.lights-camera-jackson.com

Music

http://www.kidzworld.com/entertainment/music
http://www.rollingstone.com/music/albumreviews

MP3 Players

http://reviews.cnet.com/mp3-player-buying-guide

Amusement/Theme Parks

http://themeparks.about.com/cs/attractions1/a/blbestthemed.htm

Host a Radio or TV Talk Show

Description

If you have ever heard a radio or TV talk show, you know that they provide audiences the chance to learn about a topic or issue in some depth. Sometimes, they even take questions, calls, or e-mails from audience members. You can use such a setting to share information about a topic you have studied by choosing an issue related to your topic of study that people care about, presenting the issue (often an expert is involved, sometimes two experts with differing opinions) with the host moderating the discussion.

Radio or TV talk shows are good formats for discussing current events, hot topics, controversial issues, or problem scenarios. Crime rates, limited funds, organ transplants, and computer ethics are good topics for this kind of coverage. A twist on this idea would be to interview someone from the past or future, if your topic is historical.

Presenting information this way allows you to think deeply about the issue and how it affects people in the real world; to practice communicating your ideas clearly; to interact with others to keep ideas flowing and stay focused on the main topics, and it allows people to really listen and address each other's ideas.

Planning

1. Figure out the topic for the show and read over the rubric that follows. Ask your teacher any questions you have about the criteria to be used for your evaluation.

2. Who will be the experts, and how will you prepare them for their parts? What research or background do they need to talk as an expert during the show? As the host, you will need to be prepared to support the experts if they falter a bit by asking a question that helps them out or draw them into the conversation if the other side is using up all the time. Prepare a list of questions that you will ask to

   a. Develop the base for the discussion.

   b. Give background information about the details of the issue at hand.

   c. Set up all the conversation that will follow.

   d. Re-energize the discussion during times the audience isn't responding.

3. Write out the introductory part of the show. What will you say from the moment the cameras and/or microphones are switched on? How will you

   a. greet your viewers/listeners, introduce and greet your guest(s)?

   b. ask the "setup" questions?

   c. let the dialogue continue?

4. Practice your introduction (first alone, then with someone you trust); prepare your experts, and ask your teacher to schedule your show.

5. Remember to breathe deeply, speak clearly, and have fun.

Assessing

1. Fill out a copy of the following rubric for yourself and each of your teammates; also, ask your teacher and your audience to rate your efforts.

RUBRIC

Points	4	3	2	1	SCORE
Opening of show statement	Exciting, clear introduction	Presents the topic	Gives an idea about the topic	Does not introduce topic	
Use of research	Relevant, lots of facts	Mostly relevant, some facts	Some relevancy; some facts	Lacks preparation	
Addressed other position's points	Clear, informed, effective arguments	Some clear, informed, effective arguments	Rarely clear, informed, effective arguments	Does not address other position	
Teamwork	Shared work	One person talked most of the time	One person talked all the time	No one is talking	
Use of voice, diction, gestures	Expressive, easy-to-understand	Somewhat animated, mostly able to be heard	Little animation; difficult to hear	Can't be heard; monotone	
Overall	Prepared, effective, convincing	Sometimes convincing and effective	Rarely convincing and effective	Never convincing and effective	
				TOTAL:	

2. What parts of the show went really well? Why? What could you do better next time, and how could you prepare prior to the show to make that happen?

Technology Connection

Arrange for someone to digitally record the performance for an iMovie and/or podcast. Post the performance on the school website for parents, other classes, and community members to enjoy.

Lead a Virtual Field Trip

Description

A virtual field trip is a simulated field trip using the Internet. Google Earth and webcams can take us anywhere in the world and help us learn firsthand about topics connected to almost any subject area. Museum field trips give us access to some of the world's finest collections and can help us reach new levels of understanding about whatever we are researching. In planning a trip and serving as the trip guide, you can demonstrate what you have learned about a topic as you practice the important skill of communicating your ideas to a group.

Planning

1. Using a search engine, find and evaluate virtual field trips that connect to your topic of research. Note the sites you visit and the URLs and/or links that specifically relate to your topic; note what you learned about your topic at each site.

2. You will be the tour guide for a small group of people. Answer these questions as you make your tour plan:

   a. What will be the main points that you make as you lead the tour? Come up with a provocative question for your tour members to think about as they go on the tour; the question should be related to an important point you have learned in your research. (For example, "Where in the U.S. is the most unsafe place to live due to volcanic activity?" or "As we visit Ellis Island, what similarities and differences can we see between immigration issues of the 1850s and our current immigration issues?")

   b. What questions might someone have about this topic?

   c. What background information do they need to know to make sense of what they will see on the tour?

   d. What is the most logical order to visit the different places on the tour?

   e. What humorous, awe-inspiring, interesting details or highlights will keep your audience engaged?

3. Make an outline, list, or flowchart of particular things you will point out to tour members and places you will pause and really give some background information to help people better understand what they are seeing.

4. First practice by yourself what you will say throughout the tour; then practice with another person. Time the length of the tour and make sure it does not take an entire class period. Allow time for tour members to ask questions. When you feel confident that you are prepared, let your teacher know you are ready to schedule and lead the tour.

5. Here are some museum website options:

Virtual Field Trips: *http://www.Internet4classrooms.com/vft.htm*

Utah Education Network, Build Your Own Field Trip: *http://www.uen.org/utahlink/tours*

Walter McKenzie's Innovative Teaching: *http://surfaquarium.com/IT/vft.htm*

Metropolitan Museum of Art: *http://www.metmuseum.org*

Museum of Science and Industry: *http://www.msichicago.org*

Rock and Roll Hall of Fame: *http://www.rockhall.com*

American Museum of Natural History: *http://www.amnh.org*

Sea World: *http://www.seaworld.org*

The Smithsonian Institute: *http://www.si.edu*

National Baseball Hall of Fame: *http://baseballhall.org*

George Washington's Mount Vernon: *http://www.mountvernon.org*

Biodiversity Hot Spots: *http://www.biodiversityhotspots.org/Pages/default.aspx*

Salem Witch Trials: *http://www.salemweb.com/guide/witches.shtml*

Chernobyl in Photos: *http://www.kiddofspeed.com/default.htm*

The Louvre: *http://www.louvre.fr/llv/commun/home.jsp?bmLocale=en*

Assessing

1. Ask your tour members to choose the type of reflection response they would like to make: some may write a journal reflection, a poem, or a short story; some may choose to make a mural (for example, show a panoramic view of Ellis Island with people entering the immigration office); some may choose to make an oral response (for example, one person is a newspaper reporter interviewing a family that just immigrated from another country in 1850; or someone could film another student taking on the role of an elderly person who immigrated as a child and then spent his/her life adjusting to life as an American).

2. Once the reflections are completed, study them to see what your tour members took away from their field trip. What changes would you make in leading your next field trip?

Journal or Blog

Description

A journal is a personal record of thoughts, feelings, and/or observations about something. Some people keep journals or diaries to keep a record of their daily lives. Some people keep journals during their travels so that they can remember the details of their trips for as many years as they like or to share with others. Making a journal is also a way that you can show what you have learned about a famous person; a "regular" person from a particular time period; a person traveling through a particular ecosystem recording the weather, animals, plants, and terrain; or a person who lives in a country or culture that you want to describe—journals provide endless possibilities to show learning.

Although some journals are written on paper, another option is to post your journal entries on a blog. A blog is a website that allows you to publish information and encourage discussion through comments. Many blog services allow users to upload images and videos so that blog spaces can be used as webpages. The organizing feature on blogs is a post. The posts are shown from most recent to earliest along with the author's name and date of the posting.

An example of a blog or journal that could show what you have learned about Lewis and Clark's expedition to the Pacific Ocean might begin with the start of their journey in Virginia—perhaps on the day they get their instructions from Thomas Jefferson. As Lewis and Clark proceed with preparing for the trip and then making their historic and sometimes dangerous journey, they could post (via you and your teammates) their scientific, geographic, and personal discoveries.

Planning

1. Think about the best way to use a journal or blog to share information about your project/research; will it focus on one historical figure? Will it be a famous person or a "regular" person? Will your journal start at one point and then have pauses, be picked up later, then have pauses, then be picked up again, or will it run consecutively from the day it starts? You may want to storyboard your journal—how long will it be? What main points will you cover?

2. How will you give as complete a picture as possible about everything going on at the time of the journal? Will the journal entries be written strictly from one person's point of view, or might they have read a newspaper or seen something about things happening far away in the world during the time of the journal?

3. Will there by drawings, cartoons, or humor in your journal? If you have a blog, will there be links to videos or websites? Photos?

Assessing

Use the following rubric or one that you and your teacher agree on to collect feedback about your journal project. Then discuss your project with your teacher.

Criteria for rating journal	Student	Peer	Teacher
Choice of topic			
Depth of research			
Quality of information			
Evidence of creativity			
Level of writing			
Contains factual information			

The most interesting thing I learned about this topic was

A problem I had to overcome in completing this task was

The resources I used in gathering information to do this work were

Technology Connection

If you record your journal as a blog, you can get feedback from your readers. Talk with your teacher about how blogs work, how they are monitored, what is expected of you, and the guidelines to follow as you work on the blog.

Create a blog: http://www.blogger.com

Middle school blogs: http://www.middleweb.com/mw/aaDiaries.html

Lead a Group Discussion

Description

One way to demonstrate what you have learned about a topic is to lead a large or small group discussion. By actively talking with others and drawing out their ideas, you will practice communicating what you have learned and hear alternative points of view.

Planning

1. Decide on a subject area and topic to use as a basis for discussion. Talk with your teacher about whether this is better taught through a small- or a large-group setting.

2. Prepare a simple outline of the major and minor points to cover during the discussion. This could include definition of terms or describing concepts, problems, points, events, or situations.

3. Write a series of questions to ask during the discussion.

   a. You might want to start with some simple "recall" type questions in which people are reminding each other of what happened or what the situation was. (What was the era of the dinosaurs? How many were there? When did they become extinct?)

   b. Then, you might ask open-ended questions such as "What caused that?" "Can you tell us why you think that?" "What was the effect of that?" These questions are more challenging and will get your group thinking more deeply about your topic. You will want a balance of questions to keep everyone engaged.

4. Consider using one of the following strategies to engage the discussion participants.

   a. *Discussion Guide Strategy:* Before the discussion takes place, consider giving to each student in your group a Discussion Guide that includes space to record

   - Definitions of key terms

   - Personal reactions to a concept

   - Questions that may be discussed

   - Important opinions on the topic

   b. *Human Graph Strategy:* The discussion leader prepares five different posters and places them around the room. Each poster has one term: *Strongly Agree, Agree, No Opinion, Strongly*

Disagree, or *Disagree.* Next, the leader presents other students with a series of controversial or challenging statements on a given topic. The students think about each statement carefully and then physically move to that part of the room with the sign that best describes how they feel about the statement. The leader then asks each group of students to explain its choice. As the discussion progresses, students may move from one sign to another, if the discussion gives them new insights and changes their minds.

c. *Assessment Strategy:* Prepare a rating scale for discussion participants to use in judging your effectiveness as a discussion leader and their effectiveness as a discussion member. List the criteria that the participants are to rate. You and your teacher should also rate your performance.

Assessing

1. After the discussion, write a paragraph answering these questions (1) What have I learned from today's discussion? and (2) What did I contribute to today's discussion?

2. The leader can analyze these and determine what students learned from the discussion.

3. What went well? What other questions might have been effective to include?

4. Determine how each of the discussion strategies you used worked for or against you as the discussion leader. What would you do differently or better next time?

Photo Journal

Description

Photo journals are flipbooks with pictures that tell a story. You will write accompanying words for the photos, but the effectiveness of the journal will mainly come from the power of the pictures. You can really "own" your story as you make your unique photo journal and not be held back by searching for the "correct" words. You can communicate your feelings, interpretations, and perspective through your photos.

You can use the photo journal for a lot of purposes in all the subject areas:

Math: geometric shapes, the practical uses of algebra

Social studies: history or geography of your community

Science: weather, motion, ecology, geology, plants

Language arts: autobiography, character study, inspiration for poems and stories

In making your photo journal, you will learn important technology, creativity, communication, and collaboration skills and how to properly credit multimedia sources. If you use a digital camera for this project, you can learn to adjust background colors and crop photos in shapes that help tell your story.

Planning

1. Figure out the main theme of your photo journal. What are you going to show and through whose point of view? Will it be an essay on the need to do something (The school needs a litter crew)? Will it be a process (How we raised funds for the homeless project)? Will it make a statement (The school uniform policy is not working)?

2. You can take pictures of places, objects, and people, including self-portraits; for an extra challenge, you can take photos of things as symbols or representations of other things or situations that cannot be photographed. For example, a photo of a park scene showing a group of pigeons vigorously fighting for a scrap of food might fit in a journal with a theme of competition or a journal expressing feelings about the scarcity of necessary resources.

3. You will likely take many more photos than will actually appear in your final photo journal. Select only those that tell the story and make the ideas flow. If you have taken a great photo that simply doesn't fit your theme, use it for another project. Eight or ten carefully selected photos are more effective in telling a story than a larger number of pictures lacking distinctive focus.

4. Ask your teacher whether you can learn how to change the color and tone of a photograph using Photoshop and also how to crop photos; look at some artistic

productions and websites to start thinking about cropping, placement, and framing. Consider whether you will want to use colored paper, stickers, stamps, and doodles to create borders or keep the pages simple and clean.

5. You will glue your images on cardstock paper after you

    a. Plan the layout of each page.

    b. Make color and tone changes and crops that are needed.

6. Write either *about* each of your photographs or *in response* to each of your photographs. You can write a journal entry, a poem, an essay, a story, a first-person narrative—whatever form best gets your message across. You can use more than one form of writing for your book, and you can type or handwrite your words. Carefully study your photos to see what they reveal about your topic.

7. Proofread your book and exchange work with another student for peer editing. After revising and refining your work, make your final pages and assemble your book.

8. Design a cover page.

9. Share your work with your classmates.

Assessing

Adapt the product rubric to show the criteria you think should be used to evaluate your final product, and get your teacher's approval before starting the activity.

Technology Connection

1. If Flickr (*www.flickr.com*) is available for students to use at your school, make a media album of your photo journal in slideshow format.

2. If VoiceThread (*http://voicethread.com*) is available for students to use at your school, create an interactive album of your photo journal using the microphone, text, and audio file. Organize and implement an authors' showcase for the community or translate your essay into a digital story with added background music or sound effects.

Audience Participation Report

Description

Instead of reporting in a one-way, pre-planned talk, engage your audience as you present your information: have them participate by asking questions, adding comments, or providing feedback. Here are six types of interactive reports:

1. *Outline report:* Give your audience members an outline of the information you will present in your report. After talking for about five minutes, divide your audience into small groups. Give each group two minutes to answer a question, think about an issue, or discuss a topic related to the report. Then, gather your audience back together for another five minutes of presentation and address the assigned question, point, or discussion topic in the talk.

2. *Guided report:* Give your audience members a list of three to five major points you plan to cover in your report. Ask them to listen to the report without taking any notes. At the end of the report, audience members write all the information they can recall. Then, working with partners, audience members combine their notes to reflect the report's content. In a large group review, you can fill in any gaps of information.

3. *Responsive report:* After you have decided on the topic of your report, give each person who will be in the audience a 3" x 5" file card to write an important question on the topic of the report. Then, using the questions on the file cards as guides, research and prepare your report.

4. *Demonstration report:* Prepare a five- to ten-minute talk that involves an active demonstration, experiment, or hands-on application related to your topic. Ask your audience members to respond by writing a conclusion, summary, or brief explanation of what happened and what they observed.

5. *Think/write/discuss report:* Prepare three questions to ask audience members as you move through your report. Ask the first question before the report begins, and make it a motivational question—try to get them interested in the topic. (For example: If you could do one thing in your life to prevent developing diabetes, would you do it?) In the middle of the report, ask the second question, which should require the audience members to write a short response to clarify a point or concept in the report. (For example: Do you have to totally cut out sugar from your diet to prevent diabetes? Explain your answer.) At the end of the report, ask the third question, which should ask for feedback about something they learned, something that needs further clarification, or something they misunderstood. (For example: What are two actions you can take to prevent getting Type 2 diabetes?)

6. *Bingo report:* Prepare a bingo grid with a key idea in each cell that you will discuss in your report. When audience members hear the idea discussed during the report, they cover the appropriate space with a marker. The first person to get

the cells completed across, down, or on a diagonal shouts "bingo" and wins that round. A "cover all" round is an alternative.

Planning

1. After selecting your report topic, decide which of the six formats above is the most appropriate for your chosen topic.

2. Develop a rubric to guide your work and collect feedback after your report. Ask your teacher for feedback and approval of the rubric.

3. Prepare the required material, whether it is an outline, a list of major points, a collection of completed file cards, a conclusion/summary/explanation, a series of three questions, or a set of bingo cards.

4. When you are ready, ask your teacher to schedule your report. Using your materials, involve the audience in your presentation of information.

Assessing

1. Collect the papers, questions, summaries, notes, conclusions/summaries/ explanations, or bingo cards from all audience members and analyze them to determine how successful you were in teaching the material in your report.

2. If possible, select more than one report format and try each with a small group of students to determine which one seems to work best for you and for the audience.

3. Make a list of pros and cons for each of the reporting formats outlined above from your perspective. Use this information to help you select a format to use the next time you present a report to an audience.

4. Complete your rubric and a Student Research Checklist.

Technology Connection

1. You might want to engage your audience at the start of your report by showing a short movie clip. After the clip, ask a question to get the audience thinking about the topic of your report (For example, "What might have led up to this point in the film? What might happen next?" or "What do you think about this situation?")

2. For the Bingo report, use the bingo card creator at *http://facstaff.uww.edu/jonesd/games/games_parade_buzz_word_bingo.html*

3. For the outline format use *http://www.hawaii.edu/gened/oc/outline_format.htm*

4. For the response report: have audience members blog about the report topic in advance of the presentation. Excellent free resources that will help you know what parts of your topic spark your audience's interest are *blogger.com* and *wiki.com*.

5. For tips on engaging your audience during a report, use *http://academics.hamilton.edu/occ/engagingyouraudience.pdf*

Survey, Questionnaire, or Opinion Poll

Description

Surveys, questionnaires, and opinion polls are tools used to collect data on a given subject. They allow us to learn about the feelings, beliefs, and attitudes of a smaller sample of the desired population and then, with a measure of care and luck, generalize our findings to a larger population. Keep in mind that the design of the survey, questionnaire, or opinion poll and the way questions are asked or statements are made can significantly influence the validity of the findings. Data, poorly gathered, can be misleading.

Surveys usually have a series of statements requiring the respondents to choose from a rating scale that has such response options as *strongly agree, agree, strongly disagree, disagree,* or *undecided.*

Questionnaires are more likely to have a series of questions that require the respondent to give a more detailed answer with some explanation that supports it.

Opinion polls are mostly conducted by telephone and usually focus on a single question or issue and require a simple response such as *yes, no,* or *maybe.*

Planning

1. Decide on a topic or subject that would lend itself to your actively getting input from peers, parents, community members, school personnel, etc. Then decide whether this information would best be compiled through a survey, questionnaire, or opinion poll. To help make this decision, ask yourself the following questions:

    a. Do I want to develop the topic and give the respondents a set of optional, but limited, response choices?

    b. Do I want to develop a set of questions about the topic and give the respondents more time and flexibility in answering the questions, allowing space for explanations?

    c. Do I want to develop a single question or a question with several related parts that limit the respondents to an either/or type of answer?

2. Once you have decided on a topic and a format for participant responses on the topic, you are ready to design the data-gathering survey. Some things to keep in mind for this purpose are:

    a. Define the target population or group you want to learn from.

b. Make a sampling plan to generate a randomly selected subset of the general population (how many, age, gender, etc., will give you data that you can make generalizations about).

c. Design a survey, questionnaire, or opinion poll that will give you as many responses as possible while keeping confusion to a minimum.

d. Think of some ways to get as many responses as possible. Techniques that help include putting prepaid postage on survey forms mailed out and calling at convenient times for telephone polls, keeping surveys brief and easy to use, and including a personal letter or explanation stressing the importance of the study. Rewards for completing the survey or talking on the telephone can be used as a ploy to get cooperation from potential respondents.

e. Notice any events that happened around the time of the survey that may have introduced bias or prejudice in responses.

3. Field test your survey, questionnaire, or opinion poll with a few individuals for practice and input on the quality of the data-gathering tool you created. Make revisions as needed.

4. Conduct your survey, questionnaire, or opinion pool and then compile the results using some type of tally sheet or recording system. Visually represent your results with charts and graphs. Draw conclusions from the data and share these with the respondents in some way.

Assessing

1. Study and analyze your results to determine the strengths and weaknesses of your survey, questionnaire, or opinion poll. Identify things you would do better or differently next time.

2. Analyze the process used in collecting the data. What factors led to the success of your project, and what factors seemed to interfere with it?

3. Compose a list of dos and don'ts for conducting a study using surveys, questionnaires, and/or opinion polls that others might find useful in the future.

Technology Connection

1. Put your questionnaire on SurveyMonkey, Zoomerang, Zoho Polls, FreeOnlineSurveys, or Poll Daddy. View the results and analyze them for patterns to include in your assessment.

2. If your class has a blog or wiki, use it for your survey, poll, or questionnaire.

Almanac

Description

An almanac is an interesting collection of facts and bits of advice. The first almanac, Benjamin Franklin's famous *Poor Richard's Almanac,* included factual data such as when solar or lunar eclipses would occur and pieces of advice ranging from wise sayings such as "A penny saved is a penny earned" to "It is important to plant potatoes by the dark of the moon." Almanac entries are a means of compiling data that often require knowledge of some statistics and of calculating mean, median, and mode.

Planning

1. Visit the school or public library and find examples of current almanacs. Review them to determine topics covered, numbers recorded, statistics reported, calculations applied, and types of data that would be of interest or challenging to readers. Also note what layouts or formats are most often used in the sharing of information. After noting the strengths and weaknesses of the different almanacs, create a checklist of dos and don'ts for constructing a quality almanac.

2. Themes or topics that lend themselves to an original almanac are your family, classroom, school, or community. Other possibilities for the almanac focus on a given subject area such as space travel in science or population figures of major cities in social studies.

3. To begin an original almanac, ask a series of questions that require some data gathering. If you were writing a classroom almanac, the questions might be:

    What is the average height of students in our classroom?

    How many pages a week do the students in our class read?

    What are the hobbies of the students?

    How many hours a week do members of our class watch television?

4. Once you have decided the questions, it's time to collect answers and compile and record them in an interesting, manageable way using charts, graphs, diagrams, pictures, and text.

5. Consider using spreadsheets to facilitate the calculations and publication of the data; some spreadsheets allow charts and graphs to be made from the entered data.

6. To add variety and interest, place some quotations, proverbs, jokes, riddles, words of wisdom, or anecdotes related to your topic throughout the almanac.

7. Finally, publish the almanac in booklet form, adding graphics, table of contents, title page, cover, and whatever additional pages are needed. Consider how the final product might be shared.

Assessing

Using the checklist you made after critiquing almanacs, assess the qualities of your published almanac. How does it stack up against "the real thing?" Determine what things are best about your almanac and what things you would improve if you were making an almanac again.

Technology Connection

1. A digital version of an almanac could be created on a class wiki. The almanac makers could list the topics they want to address, and contributors to the almanac could enter their information, which would be tallied or summarized by the almanac makers. The originators of each page would be responsible for ensuring that the information is accurate. The resulting almanac could be posted on the school website for other students, teachers, and parents to view. Helpful websites are

    http://pbworks.com/content/edu-classroom-teachers

    http://docs.google.com

2. Use spreadsheets and electronic chart and graph tools to display your data to make it clearly understandable to the audience.

Create a Test

Description

As you know, a test is an instrument used to measure knowledge or learning of a specific set of material. Most tests have more than one type of question. Some of the questions test for quick-memory recall of small pieces of important information or the highlights of a particular topic, while others test for understanding of larger concepts and the ability to apply these concepts when relating them to other things. Creating your own test on a unit you have recently studied in class or a project you have completed is a great way to extend your learning and help you think more deeply about the topic.

Planning

1. Multiple Choice: Make up 8 multiple choice questions based on the information the test will cover. Ask yourself what you think your teacher would expect you to know in the way of simple facts about the topic. For example, a multiple choice question about weather is:

   Which weather term describes both rain and snow?

   a. frontal system
   b. precipitation
   c. air mass
   d. humidity

2. Short Answer (fill-in-the-blank): Make up 6 short answer questions based on the same unit topic. For example: What type of cloud produces thunderstorms? (cumulonimbus)

3. Essay: Make up 2 essay questions based on the same topic. For example:

   What happens when a cold front collides with a warm front? Why?
   When a cold front collides with a warm front, the cold air mass pushes underneath the warm air mass. This often causes precipitation and sometimes storms. The reason the cold air mass slides under the warm air mass is that the cold air is more dense and heavy, and the two types of air do not mix.

4. Extra Credit: This can be whatever you want it to be. For example:

   If it rained .65 inches on Sunday, .5 inches on Monday, .25 inches on Tuesday, 0 inches on Wednesday, 0 inches again on Thursday, .3 inches on Friday, and .75 inches on Saturday, what was the average rainfall for the week?

   .35 inches

5. Answer Key: Create an answer key with the correct answers to all your test questions.

Assessing

1. When you have finished creating your test and the answer key, trade tests with another student in the class and take each other's tests. Then trade back and grade each other's tests. How did you do?

2. How did your classmate do on your test? Do you think your test was too hard or too easy?

3. If you had to do it again, what would you change about your test? Why?

Technology Connection

1. Create a crossword puzzle or word search using words and concepts from your research using *http://puzzlemaker.school.discovery.com* See if your classmates can solve the puzzle.

2. Create an online test with true-false, multiple choice, essay, or all of these at *http://school.discovery.com/quizcenter/quizcenter.html*

Role-Play Debate

Description

Participating in a debate is an excellent way to show information you have learned. Debates encourage multiple perspectives by presenting a problem with its possible solutions. They encourage lively dialogue based on facts and opinions and are by nature often argumentative. Participating in a debate will give you practice in oral presentation, strengthen your leadership and problem-solving skills, and help you see another perspective. Conducting a debate requires much preparation by the participants but is an engaging and fun experience that results in real learning.

Examples of topics that might yield different points of view are "The death penalty should be banned in the United States" "K–12 schools should ban junk food sales" "Middle schools should have mandatory drug testing for participation in extracurricular activities" "The U.S. should rely on alternative energy sources instead of fossil fuels" "Zoos do more harm than good" and "The president of the U.S. should be elected by direct vote of the people."

Planning

1. If you are using the debate to showcase a topic you have already researched, decide what related issue might produce two or more viewpoints. The debate should be balanced (have two valid positions) and researchable (information backing up each position must be available).

2. Prior to debating, each team, as a group, writes a persuasive essay including research that represents your position on the debate topic. Before you begin writing, read the writing rubric that will be used to evaluate your essay.

3. Books, current event articles in newspapers and magazines, websites and other Internet information, class notes, experts on the topic—any and all resources that would prepare you for the debate are sources you may use. Check with your teacher about whether you can consult notes or other sources during the debate.

4. In a role-play debate, the stakeholders in an issue to present their viewpoints. For example, a topic that might yield different points of view is *"Students should be required to wear uniforms to school."* Those people with differing opinions (stakeholders) might include students, parents, principals, teachers, police officers, owners of clothing stores, etc. And each of the stakeholder groups could include differing opinions.

    a. Decide your debate topic and identify all the stakeholders in the debate.

    b. Then, on an index card, write each stakeholder and give each team member a card (random drawing).

    c. Each person takes the position of the stakeholder and formulates the arguments he or she will present in a classroom debate on your topic.

d. Let your teacher know when you are ready to present so that the debate can be scheduled.

e. During the classroom debate, each stakeholder's point of view is presented, and afterward, the class asks questions of any stakeholder. The class decides whether the affirmative or negative presented the stronger case.

Assessing

1. Fill out a copy of the following rubric for yourself and each of your teammates; also, ask your teacher and your audience to rate your efforts.

DEBATE RUBRIC

POINTS	4	3	2	1	SCORE
Use of voice; rapport with audience	Exciting, easy to hear	Easy to hear, little eye contact	Hard to hear, little eye contact	Not able to be heard, no eye contact	
Arguments	Relevant, lots of facts	Mostly relevant, some facts	Some relevancy; some facts	Lacks preparation	
Addressed other position's points	Clear, informed, effective arguments	Some clear, informed, effective arguments	Rarely clear, informed, effective arguments	Does not address other position	
Teamwork	Shared work	One person talked most of the time	One person talked all the time	No one is talking	
Overall	Prepared, effective, convincing	Sometimes convincing and effective	Rarely convincing and effective	Never convincing and effective	

2. What parts of the debate went really well? Why? What could you do better next time, and how could you prepare prior to the debate to make that happen?

Technology Connection

1. Read The Big Rainforest Debate by Wendy Zweig at http://www2.lhric.org/ertc/Wendy/Wendy.htm

2. See the Middle School Public Debate Program website www.middleschooldebate.com for debate topics, a research guide, debate procedures, and resources.

Time Capsule

Description

Have you ever wished you could travel backward or forward through time? Making a time capsule enables you to do just that. You collect or make items representing a specific place in time, and you carefully label them and put them in envelopes. Colors, shapes, and sizes of envelopes may vary according to the configuration of the item to be kept. When you place objects in the time capsule, you record the name of the item on a Time Capsule Log, and all the envelopes, messages, and special items are placed in a durable container for safekeeping. The time capsule is then preserved for the future. Once time capsules are committed to a resting place for a specific period of time, a dedication speech is given at an official closing ceremony. It is also customary to say a few words on the occasion of the opening of a time capsule.

Planning

1. Consider what information on the topic you are researching could be shared by making a time capsule. Examples of time capsule projects are settings of novels (*Diary of Anne Frank*), times of interesting periods in world history, sites of famous political battles (Battle of Bunker Hill), locations of scientific adventures (Cape Canaveral for space launches). Briefly explain what topic or theme you have chosen for your time capsule and why.

2. Prepare a list of potential artifacts that could be created and placed in a time capsule to reflect the theme you have chosen. Possible items might include a newspaper article, a postage stamp, a coin, a ribbon/badge/award, a pamphlet, a drawing or diagram, a story or poem, a map, a letter, a diary entry, a handmade toy, or an illustration copied from a textbook or reference book. Keep in mind that you must design and develop whatever items are included in the time capsule.

3. List the materials needed for each artifact, the information/research required for each one, and any problems you might encounter when constructing each one.

4. Construct the artifacts, making them look as real as possible. Try to have at least eight to ten items and try to vary them in content, format, and appearance. As you complete each artifact, place it in a series of envelopes, which can be anything from a large, brown mailing envelope, to a small letter-size envelope. The envelopes can be decorated with colored pencils, stickers, ribbons, or cut-outs— or you can even make the envelopes yourself.

5. Next, is the important step of preparing a log that becomes a checklist and a brief description of all items placed in the time capsule. This serves as a table of contents for the final project. Also critical is writing a one-page outline telling

others about the author or creator of the time capsule, including the individual's name, contact information, age, date, and personal signature.

6. Finally, after all artifacts are created, identified, and placed in their respective keepsake envelopes, locate a permanent container for these items. This can be a file box, a large tin can, a shoebox, a shopping bag, or a plastic storage box. Determine the date for both storing the time capsule and then opening it. Short speeches should happen at both of these events, and could start like this:

We are gathered here to witness the passing on of a time capsule which represents the important feelings, messages, deeds, words, and treasures of _____ ...

We are gathered here to witness the opening of a time capsule containing artifacts that represent _____, as we travel back in time to learn more about this person/event/period...

Assessing

1. Use the Log Checklist for the time capsule as a basis for evaluating the quality of the items placed in the capsule. How authentic and varied were the artifacts constructed? How representative of the topic or theme were they? How well were they received by the audience? How could they have been improved?

2. Develop a rating scale to be used with the checklist and use it to rank each artifact. Write a narrative summarizing the results of your work.

3. What did you learn about yourself and your skills as you developed this project?

Challenge Box

Description

A challenge box is a container for resources and construction materials you collect that are related to a topic or theme. It provides the user with a variety of learning tools and challenging activities to help them learn more about the topic or theme. As you make the challenge box, you will have to think about the important ideas you have learned about your topic and be creative in connecting those ideas to activities and objects that others will interpret and learn from.

The challenge box can be any type of container, ranging from a file box or pizza box to a paper shopping bag or ice cream barrel. Sometimes manila envelopes and file folders can work as well. Items to place in the challenge box could be:

- reference books
- magazine articles
- pictures
- maps
- posters
- specimens
- DVDs/tapes/videos
- artifacts
- experiments
- brochures
- manipulatives
- charts/graphs/diagrams
- newspapers/catalogs
- models, puzzles
- games
- photographs

Also to be included are the instructions with descriptions of challenging activities that will help users learn more about the topic.

Planning

1. Once you know the topic or theme for the box, go on a "resource hunt" to locate as many different items as possible for the box. These items will serve as springboards and references for learning more about the topic. Each resource item in the box should be tied to a specific task outlined on the list of suggested activities.

2. After gathering the resource items, develop a list of activities that can be completed by students who are using the challenge box as a tool for learning something about the topic. Each activity should include the following sections:

    a. A materials list of specific items from the box to be used in the activity

    b. A set of directions about what to do

    c. Recording or assignment worksheets for students to write responses on

    d. Simple assessment/feedback form asking for input on how the activity turned out and what the students learned from it

3. Decide on the shape and size of the container for the challenge box items. The packaging depends, of course, on the size and extent of the resource items included as tools or references for completing the activities.

4. Write the subject area concept and/or an objective to be emphasized for each resource item in the box. What will it be used for, and how will it contribute to the learning process?

5. Write the subject area concept(s) and/or objective(s) for each activity specified in the challenge box. How do they match up with the resource items? Do they reinforce one another's purpose?

Assessing

Create a simple pre- and post-test on the topic that could be included in the contents of the challenge box. As students fill out the forms, modify the contents of the boxes based on the results.

Hands-on Report Card

Description

Although the usual printed or computerized report cards and student-led conferences are useful tools for communicating your progress, you can also demonstrate your learning through an active, hands-on activity. The hands-on report card process involves a group of students who invite their parents or guardians to the classroom on a given day. The report card demonstration requires about an hour divided into four 15-minute segments. During each 15-minute segment, you will actively demonstrate a skill that can involve a reading, writing, lab, math, or other experience, or some other relevant activity such as a computer lab application or a small-group project.

Planning

1. Your teacher will let you know the specific date, time, and place for the report card demonstrations. If you are part of a team with each person using a segment, determine what experiences or skills each person will demonstrate or display during each of the four segments.

2. Contribute to designing, constructing, and sending an invitation for the report card demonstration that explains the purpose of the visit and what your audience can expect to learn from it. If a parent or guardian cannot attend, invite another adult.

3. Make a list of all the materials you and the guests you are inviting will need and collect the materials. This includes everything from pencils and lab tools to reference books, worksheets, or recording sheets.

4. Create a simple blueprint for how you will use your allotted space during the event. How will your workspace be organized, and where will your guests be seated to best observe your part of the demonstration?

5. Estimate your activity's length and try to keep it to approximately 15 minutes duration. Time your activity and make adjustments as needed.

6. Prepare a set of questions for your guests so that after they answer them following your presentation, you will be able to tell what information they learned.

Assessing

1. Design a checklist for your activity; include all the details and actions that must be addressed before the event.

2. With input from your teacher, design a rubric that you, your guest(s), and your teacher can use to evaluate your presentation and your work.

Technology Connection

1. Create a continuous slideshow or PowerPoint that your guests can view as they wait for the event to begin. Include elements or background from each of the demonstrations they will see; if possible, find connections between the topics to help your audience think about them in new ways.

2. If you use technology for any part of your project, clearly explain how the technology impacted the task so that any audience members not familiar with that technology can picture how it worked.

Problem-Solving Party

Description

Having effective skills and strategies for problem solving is essential in today's world. To add a bit of interest and challenge to learning problem-solving skills, teachers and students can make problem solving the theme for a party in the classroom. To make such a party successful requires much effort. A variety of problem-solving situations that can serve as the entertainment and the action for the party have to be created. Involving students in creating and/or selecting the problems based on what they have learned about a particular topic will motivate them to really look at the main ideas they have been studying and to look for real-world applications and ways to explain what they have learned to their classmates. Encourage students to first focus on the problem-solving situations and then tackle the normal party planning details of date, time, invitations, decorations, and treats. This activity can best be carried out by a small group or a small team.

Planning

1. Brainstorm and research a number of problem-solving tasks that could be set up in learning stations around the room with one or more tasks assigned to each station. Each station should include clear directions for each problem-solving challenge and whatever resource materials are required to attack the problem presented. Consider providing an answer key for self-checking of accuracy. Remember to prepare a wide variety of problem-solving activities so that early finishers can complete another station. Sketch the floor plan for the learning stations and label each station with a brief list by title of the problem-solving tasks to be placed at each station.

2. Decide the better way to organize the stations:

    a. One main topic could be the theme for all the problems.
        For example: if the topic is Medieval Times, you could have
        a math station, a language arts station,
        a science station, a social studies station, etc.

    b. Each station could have a different topic (castles,
        jousting, war/peace, family life, social classes) with
        activities from each subject area at each one.

3. Examples of problem-solving activities:

    Math: word or logic problems

    Language arts: crosswords, word finders, sequence puzzles

    Science: experiments, laboratory mysteries, model making

    Social studies: maps, famous people riddles

4. Examples of skills:

> Make a table, chart, or graph of the data provided.
>
> Make an organized list.
>
> Make an educated guess and then check references for accuracy.
>
> Identify a pattern or hidden solution.
>
> Draw a picture or diagram.
>
> Work backward.
>
> Work a simpler problem as a warm-up first.
>
> Use logical reasoning and deduction.
>
> Brainstorm ideas.

5. Prepare a detailed list of all aspects of the party that can be used as a checklist for marking off tasks as they are completed.

6. Select a date, time, and place for the party. Be sure to clear arrangements with everyone to be involved in the party or affected by it.

7. Decide on a color scheme and design invitations and decorations for the event around the theme or colors chosen. Think about incorporating some problem-solving symbols or graphics at the stations and around the room. Perhaps math, grammar, science, or social studies symbols could be used. Sketch the party invitation, decorations, and list the food to be served.

8. Design a simple survey that party guests can complete; have them give you feedback on the party theme and the problem-solving tasks.

Assessing

1. Using the outline/checklist, lead a discussion with the participants on what worked and what could have gone better. Identify specific lessons learned.

2. Analyze the surveys completed by your guests. What did they like, and what did they think of the different activities?

3. Using the list of problem-solving tasks and the survey results, write your conclusions.

Technology Connection

Take some movie clips or still photos during the party that highlight the concepts and lessons learned during the problem-solving party. Edit them and create a presentation that can be shared with parents, other classes, and the community via the school website.

Photography Field Trip

Description

All communities offer unlimited sites for meaningful field trips. A list of suggested sites appears below. The keys to any successful outing are the planning before the trip, the activities during the trip, and the post-trip follow-up activities. When students create photo essays, they have both a personal (because they are choosing the perspective) and academic outlet for the field trip experience. Students can photograph events and record information about each picture in the form of descriptions, explanations, observations, and/or summaries of sites and situations. Cameras can be brought from home, borrowed from the school, or included in the cost of the field trip if throwaway cameras are used.

Planning

1. Make the arrangements with the site:

   - Locate the contact's name and phone number.

   - Establish the date and time of visit.

   - Prepare the materials/directions to be given to students and chaperones.

   - Select which areas of the site will be visited and the availability of a guide.

   - Research Web materials about the site.

   - Invite a person from the site to visit your classroom.

   - Confirm the day before the trip.

   - Discuss safety and behavioral expectations for the trip.

   - Discuss photo essay guidelines.

2. Potential field trip sites:

Botanical garden	Fire station
Cemetery	Historic sites
City hall	Hotel
College campus	Humane Society
Construction site	Junk dealer
Courthouse	Recycling center
Dairy	Landfill
Factory	Library
Farm	Monuments

Museum	Ship, ferry
Newspaper	Sports stadium
Orchard	State capitol
Orchestra	Theater
Parents' businesses	TV station
Planetarium	Utility
Police station	Veterinarian
Printing company	Animal refuge
Radio station	Zoo

3. Select a field trip site that has relevance, interest, and potential for enhancing a topic in your curriculum. Once the place, time, and date are decided, prepare students for the trip by having them complete one or more of the following tasks:

   a. Stimulate ideas about the trip using Internet sources, reference books, videos, brochures, or artifacts.

   b. Design a series of scavenger hunt questions that will help note locations of important items or details.

   c. Discuss with students expectations for their photo essays and possible settings/activities that would make interesting photographs. Encourage students to take photos of what interests them but ones that at the end, will have a theme or thread tying the photos together and to the content they are studying. Giving them examples of what you consider good work will help them meet your expectations.

   d. Invite a professional photographer or a person who takes great photos, perhaps a teacher or even a student with a good eye, to speak to the class about how to take good photos.

4. During the trip, encourage the participants to do one or more of the following:

   a. Work in pairs to complete the scavenger hunt questions.

   b. Take pictures of several interesting and informative people, displays, exhibits, events, or facilities.

   c. Record several varied pieces of information for each photo such as historical data, numerical data, cultural data, etc.

5. Following the trip, have students

   a. Review their digital images (or developed film images).

   b. Arrange them in a logical sequence for display and dialogue.

   c. Place them in an album (purchased or constructed from poster board and construction paper).

   d. Create a model, quiz, Jeopardy-type game, chart, poster, or booklet of information learned on the trip.

Assessing

1. Study the photos in the finished album along with the recorded information about each one, and decide how you will rate each entry on the basis of these criteria:

    a. Choice of subject area for photo

    b. Quality of photo itself

    c. Relevance and completeness of information for photograph

    d. Other (to be determined by student and/or teacher)

Technology Connection

Using digital cameras will greatly increase the ease and flexibility of manipulating, storing, and sharing the photos.

Twenty-Five More Ways
For Students To Share Information

1. Collect oral history information about (a) relatives who live in other places; (b) local business entrepreneurs; (c) a senior citizen; (d) someone who fought in a war; (e) someone who volunteers; (f) survivors of a natural disaster; (g) an immigrant who values life in the United States; (h) a religious or political leader in the community.

2. Read an account of a current event and also watch a news account of the same event. With your team members, create a Venn diagram of how the two accounts are similar and different. Each you should then individually write a summary of your understanding of what actually occurred. For an extra challenge, observe news coverage of the same event as reported by two different countries. Great resources are at *www.newseum.org*—where newspapers from around the world are online everyday (Spencer, 2008, p. 31).

3. Artistically interpret a song, dance, movie, television show, period of history, poem, mathematical formula or theory, scientific discovery, archeological dig, or wonder of the world. Perform or share it with others.

4. Draw a detailed picture of a tree, storm, sunset, rain forest, desert, political rally, battle, piece of architecture, snowflake, myth, tall tale, legend, chemical reaction, life cycle, experiment, historical event, museum exhibit, or act of kindness.

5. Volunteer your services to a library, museum, hospital, senior friendship center, school, community agency, daycare center, church, the Humane Society, or the Red Cross.

6. Make a booklet of riddles, stories, quotations, recipes, fads and fashions, ideas, unusual words, symmetry in nature, architectural features, history-in-the-making, environmental problems, happy moments, people, scenes from city or country life, unsung heroes, or favorite places.

7. Construct photo files of cut-out magazine pictures that are pasted onto 5" x 8" index cards. Use these to play memory games, sorting/classifying games, what comes before and after games, imagination games, or role-playing games.

8. Use a digital camera to take photos of three examples of symmetry around your home; take portrait photos and write character descriptions based on them; take photos of interesting sites and write real-life math problems based on them; or find historical sites in your area to create a photo essay related to the content you are studying (Spencer, 2008, p. 60).

9. Make a book of lists based on a common theme such as vocabulary, grammar, literature, numbers, geometry, history, geography, human body, oceanography, stars and planets, weather, rocks and minerals, music, art, or sports.

10. Design a sign advertising a story you have read, promoting tourism in your community, publicizing a national monument in another country, promoting health and fitness, promoting the artwork of Renoir or the music of Mozart. Design a sign that could have been useful to Julius Caesar, angered Abraham Lincoln, carried by a protestor of the Stamp Act of 1765, helped preserve a specific endangered species, placed on a spacecraft to Mars, located only at the South Pole.

11. Create a flow chart that shows how to use the Internet, how to prepare for a job interview, how a bill becomes a law, how to make a bar or line graph, how to solve a word problem, how sedimentary rocks are formed, how to test for acids and bases, how to elect a president, how to study for a test, the sequence of events in a novel, or the major events that led up to the Revolutionary War.

12. Design a set of fact cards, trading cards, or Who Am I cards based on a theme or topic such as world leaders, famous artists or musicians, interesting math facts, geographical features, historical events, important inventions, sports, heroes, unsolved mysteries, unpopular villains, or national monuments/symbols.

13. Organize a collection of rocks, shells, buttons, autographs, model airplanes, calendars, masks, coins, stamps, pencils, napkins/match book covers, postcards, business cards, photographs, posters, record album covers, or paper dolls. Organize a hobby fair to show your collection and encourage sharing of other collectibles.

14. Use a computer to write a story or play, create a newsletter, make personal stationery and labels, design a car, catalog your books, set up a dictionary, compile a bibliography of kid-centered websites, review software, or play a game.

15. Prepare and give a speech to celebrate, inform, persuade, narrate, criticize, debate, or promote something.

16. Redesign and/or improve an umbrella, tent, bicycle, broom, camera, snow shovel, yo-yo, room you stay or work in, cereal, book cover, shopping mall, or video game.

17. Design a set of cut-outs or paper dolls that depict book characters, historical periods, tall tale figures, monsters, legendary heroes, movie or television stars, Walt Disney characters, or comic book people.

18. Design a series of science or physics experiments using children's toys as the focus of each one. For example, what could you teach kids about physics or science using a yo-yo, kite, a bicycle, a skateboard, a set of blocks, a toy boat, a Frisbee, or a rubber ball?

19. Create a personal exhibit of your original art, original writing, original science experiments, original research, original puzzle designs, or original musical compositions/ collages/tapes. Produce a brochure that gives information about the exhibit.

20. Plan a mini-conference for students in your classroom or school. Decide on a topic or theme of interest to kids. Then develop plans for publicity, speakers, panels, debates, presentations, exhibits, demonstrations, hand-outs, decorations, and food/snacks.

21. Present a mock trial or panel discussion to share information orally. Mock trials that include key courtroom roles and procedures can be staged to interpret fairy tales, myths, legends, or historical events. Panel discussions are popular formats for discussing current events, hot topics, controversial issues, or problem scenarios. Crime rates, limited terms/funds for elected officials, organ transplants, or computer ethics are good topics for coverage in this manner.

22. Build a construction model or invention to apply knowledge and skills while making visual representations and replicas of key concepts combined with your personal interpretations. Plan an invention parade or trade fair to exhibit the models for widespread viewing by spectators.

23. Design a how-to manual and do a hands-on demonstration to communicate technical know-how to others. Computers and other electronic tools are practical springboards for teaching new skills and concepts to those who have not yet mastered them. "Learning by doing" is most effective when it is accompanied by written directions, diagrams, charts, graphs, drawings, or sketches that further explain what is being shown manually.

24. Research how to make many different types of puppets (finger puppets, paper bag/plate puppets, sock puppets, papier-mâché puppets, stick puppets, marionettes, etc.). Make a number of these puppets, and use them to put on a puppet show to teach or tell about something.

25. With a partner, create a chart based on a question or problem based on major concepts you have been studying. For example: Create a chart that compares one of the reform movements of the mid-1800s (abolition, temperance, women's rights, education) with a contemporary issue (abortion rights, undocumented immigrants, smoking, environment). Think about people involved, tactics, or points of view. With your partner discuss the issues, create the chart, and then post it. As partners, share your ideas as the class discusses the chart. (Spencer, 2008, p. 60).

References

Elliott, L. (2011). *Teach like a techie: 20 tools for reaching the digital generation.* Peterborough, NH: Crystal Springs Books.

Spencer, J. (2008). *Everyone's invited! Interactive strategies that engage young adolescents.* Westerville, OH: National Middle School Association.

Part III

Additional Resources

I. Ten Other Ways To Measure What Students Know

1. Conduct a Hollywood Squares Review. Make up a set of questions pertaining to subject matter and simulate the tic-tac-toe game show format used on this old television show. Place three chairs in a row for students to sit on; place three students on the floor in front of the chairs; and place three students standing behind the chairs. Give each student "celebrity" a card with an "X" printed on one side and a "0" on the other side. Choose contestants who in turn pick a member of the "celebrity" squares to answer the game's questions. Contestants then "agree" or "disagree" to the panel's response as they try to form a tic-tac-toe. Remaining students can also be given cards that say "agree" or "disagree" on them to participate in the decision making.

2. Prepare a set of Question Cards and set of corresponding Answer Cards. Shuffle the cards and distribute randomly to students. Instruct students to find their matching cards and then collectively use them to challenge classmates by reading their questions aloud and asking for responses. Be sure to clarify valid answers so that everyone understands the concept.

3. Create a set of Response Cards for each student. These cards could contain letters A, B, or C for multiple choice questions, T or F for true/false questions, or numerical ratings such as 1 to 5 for rank order questions. Read a set of statements and ask students to respond by holding up the card of their choice. Again, work to achieve an understanding of the idea or information in question.

4. Use iPhoto, PowerPoint, Keynote, or other software to create slide shows related to the vocabulary, concepts, events, or people the class is studying. The slide shows will help students make mental pictures of the words they have learned. Divide the class into sections and give each section a different role during the slide show. For example, one section can write what they observe, one can identify and list important vocabulary words, and one can prepare questions the slides raise. At the end of the slide show, the students can share lists and begin making a word wall for the unit (Spencer, 2008, p. 5).

5. Give each student an index card that contains information or an example that fits into one or more categories of a topic or unit they have studied in detail. Ask students to mill around the room and find others whose cards fit the same category. You may announce the categories beforehand or allow the student to discover them. Have students with the same category of cards present themselves to the rest of the group.

6. Collect assorted magazines, journals, newspapers, and articles; then have students create an Assessment Collage that summarizes what they have learned on a given topic. Ask each student to include a list that briefly tells what each item in the collage represents.

7. Group students into two circles, an inner circle and an outer circle. Prepare a set of questions on a given unit of study and post them on an overhead, a bulletin board, or a chart stand. Instruct both circles to move slowly in opposite directions until given the cue to stop, which can be the blow of a whistle, the flick of a light, or the cessation of music playing on a tape. Ask students to discuss the answer to the first question with the person in front of them. After a minute or two, repeat the process until all questions have been addressed and all persons have had a chance to dialogue with a different partner.

8. Prepare a Take Home Test for students to complete that requires the use of multiple sources such as textbook sections, class notes, worksheets, lecture outlines, informal quizzes, or portfolio artifacts as references to complete the test.

9. Prepare an In-Classroom Test for students to complete that allows them to use one 3" x 5" or 4" x 6" file card of notes prepared ahead of time as "cheat sheets" during the taking of the test.

10. Ask students to create a "Visual Display" of the major concepts or ideas they have learned during a unit of study.

2. Using Williams' Taxonomy for Researched-Based Tasks

Williams' Taxonomy of Creative Thought involves the act of imagining, visualizing, or conceptualizing something new and original. It requires an attitude, outlook, perspective, or view that breaks established rules or manipulates knowledge or experience in uncommon ways. The Williams model has been widely used in classrooms to develop creativity in students. The chart given here summarizes the eight levels of the taxonomy and includes sample cue words for each of those levels.

FLUENCY

Enables the learner to generate a great many ideas, related answers, or choices in a given situation. Sample Cue Words: *Generating oodles, lots, many ideas.*

FLEXIBILITY

Lets the learner change everyday objects to generate a variety of categories by taking detours and varying sizes, shapes, quantities, time limits, requirements, objectives, or dimensions in a given situation. Sample Cue Words: *Generating varied, different, alternative ideas.*

ORIGINALITY

Causes the learner to seek new ideas by suggesting unusual twists to change content or by coming up with clever responses to a given situation. Sample Cue Words: *Generating unusual, unique, new ideas.*

ELABORATION

Helps the learner stretch by expanding, enlarging, enriching, or embellishing possibilities that build on previous thoughts or ideas. Sample Cue Words: *Generating enriched, embellished, expanded ideas.*

RISK TAKING

Enables the learner to deal with the unknown by taking chances, experimenting with new ideas, or trying new challenges. Sample Cue Words: *Experimenting with and exploring ideas.*

COMPLEXITY

Permits the learner to create structure in an unstructured setting or to build a logical order in a given situation. Sample Cue Words: *Improving and explaining ideas.*

CURIOSITY

Encourages the learner to follow a hunch, question alternatives, ponder outcomes, and wonder about options. Sample Cue Words: *Pondering and questioning ideas.*

IMAGINATION

Allows the learner to visualize possibilities, build images in his or her mind, picture new objects, or reach beyond the limits of the practical. Sample Cue Words: *Visualizing and fantasizing ideas*

3. Using Revised Bloom's Taxonomy for Research-Based Tasks

Revised Bloom's Taxonomy is a useful tool that students can use to help them focus on learning tasks when researching and responding to a given assignment in any subject. It consists of six levels that are arranged in a hierarchy with *Remembering* tasks requiring the lowest level of thinking and doing and *Creating* tasks requiring the highest level of thinking and doing.

1. One must be able to function at each level before moving to the next level.

2. Each level of the taxonomy has a set of suggested verbs, behaviors, skills, or tasks associated with it for the purposes of guiding the student in the selection, planning, and preparation of an assigned product, performance, or portfolio item.

3. All students can function at all levels of the taxonomy providing the content being studied is at the appropriate reading and operational level of the student.

4. Students should limit the number of specified verbs, behaviors, skills, or tasks used in any given assignment so as to make the assignment manageable.

Bloom's Taxonomy of Critical Thought

Remembering: Retrieving, recognizing, Sample Verbs: *Acquire, define, find, follow directions, identify, know, label, list, match, memorize, name, quote, read, record, select, state, write.*

Understanding: constructing meaning. Sample Verbs: *Account for, classify, compare, demonstrate, differentiate, explain, give examples, give in own words, group, illustrate, infer, interpret, outline, paraphrase, predict, recognize, represent, retell, show, simplify, summarize.*

Applying: or using information. Sample Verbs: *Apply, compute, construct, convert, demonstrate, derive, develop, discover, discuss, examine, execute, experiment, generalize, implement, interview, investigate, model, participate, perform, plan, prepare, produce, prove, solve, utilize.*

Analyzing: Break the information down into its component parts; determine how the parts relate to one another and to an overall structure or purpose. Sample Verbs: *Analyze, categorize, classify, compare, contrast, criticize, debate, determine, diagram, differentiate, discover, discriminate, draw conclusions, examine, generalize, infer, illustrate, organize, relate, search.*

Evaluating: Make judgments based on criteria and standards. Sample Verbs: *Argue, award, check, critique, defend, interpret, judge, measure, select, set standards, test, verify.*

Creating: Combine elements to form a coherent or functional whole. Sample verbs: *Arrange, combine, blend, create, deduce, devise, generate, organize, plan, present, produce, rearrange, reorganize, rewrite, synthesize.*

Source: http://faculty.chass.ncsu.edu/slatta/hi216/learning/bloom.htm

4. Using the Multiple Intelligences for Research-Based Tasks

Dr. Howard Gardner's concept of multiple intelligences can provide both the teacher and the student with a wonderful structure for researching, reporting, and presenting information. This theory allows one to choose any topic, gather data and facts on that topic, and then summarize and share those topic ideas through eight different intelligences. The chart on the next page briefly defines all eight of the identified intelligences, suggests strategies or information-sharing projects, and cites specific career choices to illustrate each one.

When using the Multiple Intelligences as an organizing structure for product, performance, or portfolio tasks, one should consider the following questions:

1. What tasks require students to write, speak, or read? (Verbal/Linguistic Application)

2. What tasks require students to engage in problem solving, logical thought, or calculations? (Logical/Mathematical Application)

3. What tasks require students to create images or visual aids and to analyze colors, textures, forms, or shapes? (Visual/Spatial Application)

4. What tasks require students to employ body motions, manipulations, or hands-on approaches to learning? (Body/Kinesthetic Application)

5. What tasks require students to incorporate music, rhythm, pitch, tones, or environmental sounds in their work? (Musical/Rhythmic Application)

6. What tasks require students to work in groups and to interact with other people? (Interpersonal Application)

7. What tasks require students to express personal feelings, insights, beliefs, and self-disclosing ideas? (Intrapersonal Application)

8. What tasks require students to consider the influences of the environment, the ecology, and the phenomena of Mother Nature? (Naturalist/Physical Application)

INTELLIGENCE	DESCRIPTION	STRATEGIES	CAREERS
Verbal/Linguistic	Intelligence of words and production of language	Journal writing, making speeches, storytelling, reading	Novelists, comedians, journalists
Logical/Mathematical	Intelligence of numbers, logic, and inductive reasoning	Developing outlines, creating codes, calculating, problem solving	Accountants, lawyers, computer programmers
Visual/Spacial	Intelligence of pictures, mental images, and sight	Drawing, using guided imagery, making mind maps, making charts	Architects, mechanical engineers, map makers
Body/Kinesthetic	Intelligence of physical self, control of one's body movements, and learning by doing	Role playing, dancing, playing games, using manipulatives	Athletes, inventors, mechanics
Musical/Rhythmic	Intelligence of recognition and use of rhythmic or tonal patterns and sensitivity to sounds from the environment	Singing, performing, writing, composing, playing instruments, performing choral readings	Musicians, advertising designers, composers
Interpersonal	Intelligence of people skills, communication skills, and collaborative skills	Working with mentors and tutors, participating in interactive projects, using cooperative learning	Teachers, politicians, religious leaders
Intrapersonal	Intelligence of the inner self, intuition, and emotions	Using learning centers, participating in self reflection tasks, using higher-order reasoning, taking personal inventories	Psychiatrists, counselors, entrepreneurs
Naturalist/Physical	Intelligence of nature, environment, ecosystems, and one ruled by Mother Nature	Observing, digging, planting, displaying, sorting, uncovering, and relating	Conservationists, environmentalists, hikers, bird watchers

5. Criteria and Questions to Consider When Designing Rubrics

When you and your teacher are designing rubrics to evaluate your portfolio, performance, or products, you may want to consider the following criteria and questions.

Portfolio

PORTFOLIO ASSESSMENT CRITERIA TO CHOOSE FROM:

1. Overall organization with table of contents
2. Rationale or process stated for selection of work samples
3. Variety of artifacts or work samples represented
4. Clarity or purpose stated
5. Thoroughness evident
6. Multiple resources represented
7. Time management evident
8. Understanding of portfolio concept demonstrated
9. Personal reflections included
10. Creativity present
11. Learning goals emphasized
12. Quality of presentation acceptable

SOME PORTFOLIO QUESTIONS TO PONDER.

1. What artifacts do you value the most? the least?
2. What artifacts best show your strength as a learner?
3. What artifacts best show your versatility or adaptability?
4. What artifacts best show your creativity?
5. What does your portfolio tell others about you as a learner?
6. What does your portfolio tell others about you as a risk taker?
7. How would I most like my portfolio to be evaluated? Do I want a single grade given to the entire portfolio? Do I want each piece of work in the portfolio to be graded separately on the basis of predetermined criteria for each assignment? Do I not want a grade on the portfolio because it is primarily a tool to allow me to see my personal growth and development over the course? Do I want grades on only a few pieces from the final portfolio that best represent my body of work over a marking period or semester?

Performance

PERFORMANCE ASSESSMENT CRITERIA TO CHOOSE FROM:

1. Orderly flow and sequence of ideas
2. Effective use of motions and gestures
3. Energetic, fluid performance
4. Dramatic flair observed
5. Expressive voice and clear enunciation
6. Steady pace in presenting ideas
7. Adequate volume in projection of voice
8. Good eye contact
9. Significant information included
10. Accurate information provided
11. Correct usage of vocabulary
12. Evidence of adequate practice and rehearsal
13. Overall oral delivery of text
14. Rapport with audience
15. Visual aide(s) used effectively
16. Appropriate use of notes or cue cards

Performance questions to ponder.

1. Did I do a good job in my background research?
2. Did I include proper use of specialized vocabulary?
3. How did I connect with the audience?
4. Did I sequence my information well?
5. Did I adequately identify main points and summarize details?
6. Did I open and close my performance with memorable statements or strategies?
7. How would I improve my performance next time?
8. What advice would I give someone who is preparing for a performance assessment activity?

Product

PRODUCT ASSESSMENT CRITERIA TO CHOOSE FROM:

1. Depth and quality of research
2. Clarity of thought and ideas
3. Organization
4. Appropriate understanding of concepts through generalizations, interpretations, and conclusions
5. Grammatically correct sentences and paragraphs
6. Appropriate focus on topic
7. Well organized introduction, body, and conclusion
8. Factually correct
9. Accuracy of terms, definitions, and information
10. Adequate length
11. Attractiveness
12. Flowing sequence of ideas presented
13. Contains clarifying charts, graphs, pictures, diagrams, maps, or visuals as needed
14. Resources varied
15. Resources cited

PRODUCT QUESTIONS TO PONDER.

1. Did I choose a manageable topic to research?
   Did I clearly define the topic being examined? How do I know?
2. How authentic and varied were my sources of information?
3. Did I adequately paraphrase the data researched and cited so that the ideas were expressed in my own words? How did I do this?
4. How much did I enjoy my work on this project?
5. What things did I learn from this project? What new skills, ideas, or concepts?
6. How well did I manage my time doing this project?
7. Just how much was I committed to making this project a quality effort?
8. What evidence of pride or personal satisfaction is evident in this project?

Cooperative Learning

COOPERATIVE LEARNING ASSESSMENT CRITERIA TO CHOOSE FROM:

1. Active listening consistent
2. Application of social skills evident
3. Consistently staying on task
4. Making regular and consistent contributions
5. Appropriate use of body language
6. Responsible for own behavior
7. Carried out assigned role responsibilities
8. Shared in planning, research, and completion of assigned task
9. Evidence of enjoyment, pride, satisfaction with process
10. Independence of ideas and efforts
11. Overall academic goal achievement evident
12. Entire group involved
13. Worked well without supervision
14. Followed instructions

COOPERATIVE LEARNING QUESTIONS TO PONDER.

1. What do you like best about working with others in a group?
2. What is most difficult for you when working in a group?
3. What makes for a good cooperative learning group experience?
4. What cooperative learning skills did you practice today?
5. What social skill do you need to work harder on?
6. What did you do to help your group complete the assigned task?
7. What could you do the next time to be a better team member?
8. How well did I share my ideas with other members of the group?
9. What would my team members say about my contributions to the group's assigned task?
10. How do you feel about your group's accomplishment and functioning today?

Rubrics for Assessment (University of Wisconsin–Stout, May 2011) offers a wealth of rubrics organized by products, performances, Web 2.0 tools, skills, technology, processes, research, cooperative learning, etc., at *http://www.uwstout.edu/soe/profdev/rubrics.cfm#game*

6. Sample Rubric For Product Assessment

CONTINUUM FORMAT

NAME: _____   TYPE OF PRODUCT: _____

DATE OF PRODUCT: _____   COMPLETION DATE OF PRODUCT: _____

	Off Target	Near Miss	Very Close	Bull's Eye
Manageable topic				
Evidence of quality research				
Contains factual information				
Well written				
Elements of creativity				
Application of higher-order thinking skills				
Adequate length				

COMPLETE THESE STARTER STATEMENTS.

The most enjoyable part of creating this product was _____

_____

The most interesting thing I learned about this topic was _____

_____

A problem I had to overcome in completing this task was _____

_____

The resources I used in gathering information to do this work were _____

_____

If I did this project again, I would change _____

_____

SIGNED _____
STUDENT SIGNATURE

7. Sample Rubric for Performance Assessment

RATING SCALE FORMAT

STUDENT'S NAME: _____ TYPE OF PRODUCT: _____

NAME OF INDIVIDUAL RATING PERFORMANCE: _____

TOPIC/THEME/SUBJECT AREA OF PERFORMANCE: _____

RATING SCALE USED IN ASSESSING PERFORMANCE:

Outstanding	Excellent	Good	Fair	Unsatisfactory
5	4	3	2	1

Criteria for Rating Performance	Student	Teacher
1. Choice of topic/theme		
2. Depth of research		
3. Organization of ideas; key points clear		
4. Quality of information; required content included		
5. Calm, confident, no distracting behaviors; every word was heard.		
6. Constant eye contact with audience; occasional glances at notes; effective gestures		
7. Engages audience with lots of feeling in voice; emotion, passion, excitement, sadness evident		
8. Evidence of creativity		

If I were rating this performance, I would give myself a(n) _____ (letter grade) because _____

_____

_____

8. Sample Rubric for Portfolio Assessment

CHECKLIST FORMAT

SUBMITTED BY: _____ ON: _____
STUDENT'S NAME   DATE

SUBMITTED TO: _____ ON: _____
TEACHER'S NAME   DATE

PLEASE REVIEW MY PORTFOLIO FOR THE FOLLOWING:

Name of item	Yes	No
1. Adequate storage container		
2. Table of contents listing artifacts		
3. Clear Organization		
4. Inclusion of ten artifacts listed below		
A.		
B.		
C.		
D.		
E.		
F.		
G.		
H.		
I.		
J.		
5. Student reflections for each item		
6. Self-assessment comments by student		
7. Formal assessment comments by teacher		
8. Peer review comments by classmates		
9. Feedback comments by parent/guardian		

Part IV

Teacher Study Materials

This section provides a sampling of professional literature highlighting examples of educators using authentic assessments in both formative and summative ways. These educators are continually trying to define what student performance means—they know it's more than what paper and pencil tests reveal.

By discussing the following materials, your faculty, team, and/or learning community can support each other in improving student performance by varying the means students use to achieve comparable performance. The two materials included in this section complement each other and can be used to good advantage in tandem.

The first reading, "Authentic Assessment of 21st Century Literacies" features the essential questions about authentic assessment answered with real-life examples of teachers dealing with those questions. Following the questions and answers are prompts to guide your study group's discussions.

The second article, "Formative and Summative Authentic Assessment" provides you with background on the nature of formative and summative assessment, information about balancing the two forms, and strategies for implementing assessments. Following the textual information are prompts to help you analyze your present assessment efforts and guide you in deciding your future assessment goals.

Literature Reading #1:
Authentic Assessment of 21st Century Literacies

Why do we need to develop alternative forms of assessment?

This era of standards and high stakes testing has certainly placed new challenges before middle school faculties to improve student performance. One of these challenges is to define what student performance means. Many of us believe in our guts that performance is really more than what paper and pencil tests test. But what? And what can we do about it?

The second big challenge is one we may not even be aware of in all the hubbub about yearly raising test scores. Ends and means (outcomes and the processes used to accomplish those outcomes) are different things that we sometimes confuse. We cannot specify both simultaneously!

You can specify either outcomes or the means to achieve them, but not both. We can decide that a curricular activity is important for every student to experience, but then we cannot control the student outcomes. For example, we can decide that every student should read a particular novel (for example, *The Adventures of Tom Sawyer*). By so doing, we can provide a common cultural experience for all learners, but the student learning outcomes of such a decision will vary greatly among students. For some this experience will be an easy read; others will struggle with decoding the novel. Each student will bring different background experiences to this reading assignment and will take different things out of it.

On the other hand, we can specify that students will be able to perform tasks at a certain level of competence. However, if our goal is to get all learners to the same point at about the same time (the requirement placed on us by the *No Child Left Behind Act*) then to be successful, we must vary the means for getting students to the same point. Because students vary according to previous knowledge, motivation, ability, at-risk factors, family background, social maturity and so forth, we cannot provide the same means to get students to the same ends or outcomes.

Failing to realize this distinction is causing some of us to make a fatal flaw in our instructional planning when we attempt get all students to perform at the same level by leading them through the same prepackaged, or even locally developed, learning experiences.

Erb, 2003

What are some limitations of traditional testing?

Rothstein (2000) used a baseball example to question the veracity of using a single high stakes test to measure a student's knowledge:

> Mike Piazza, batting .332, could win this year's Most Valuable Player award. He has been good every year, with a .330 career batting average, ... and a member of each All Star team since his rookie season. The Mets reward Piazza for this high achievement, at the rate of $13 million a year.

But what if the team decided to pay him based not on overall performance but on how he hit during one arbitrarily chosen week? How well do one week's at-bats describe the ability of a true .330 hitter?

Not very. Last week Piazza batted only .200. But in the second week of August he batted .538. If you picked a random week this season, you would have only a 7-in-10 chance of choosing one in which he hit .250 or higher. (p. B11)

So I'm the valedictorian. Number one. But, what separates me from number two, three, four, five, six, 50, or 120? Nothing but meaningless numbers. All these randomly assigned numbers reflect nothing about the true character of an individual. They say nothing … about desire or will. Nothing about values or morals. Nothing about intelligence. Nothing about creativity. Nothing about heart. Numbers cannot and will not ever be able to tell you who a person really is.

French 2003

What does the research tell us about how grading and reporting practices benefit students and encourage learning?

Although there are a multitude of studies with often incongruous results, researchers do appear to agree on the following points:

a. Grading and reporting are not essential to instruction. Teachers do not need grades or reporting forms to teach, and students can and do learn without them.

b. No one method of grading and reporting serves all purposes well.

c. Grading and reporting will always involve some degree of subjectivity. Regardless of the method used, assigning grades or reporting on student learning is inherently subjective. In addition, the more detailed the reporting method and the more analytic the process, the more likely subjectivity will influence results (Ornstein, 1994).

d. Grades have some value as rewards, but no value as punishments.

e. Grading and reporting should always be done in reference to learning criteria, never "on the curve." Using the normal probability curve as a basis for assigning grades typically yields greater consistency in grade distributions from one teacher to the next. The practice, however, is detrimental to both teaching and learning.

Guskey, 1996

What things other than those on standardized tests should be assessed?

It is a chilly fall morning in Snow Lake, a town of 1300 people in northern Manitoba, Canada. Two sixth grade boys from Kerr School trudge off down the road toward the lakeshore. They are laden with two digital still cameras, a digital camcorder, and several notebooks. This is a school day, and they are off by themselves to document the life of a local commercial fisherman. Their teacher, Clarence Fisher, has arranged for them to spend the morning with the man who lives and works in their town. Earlier, the boys had interviewed the fisherman on the phone; this morning the boys are recording their experiences on the two digital still cameras and one video camcorder. They also write notes in their paper notebooks. When the boys get back, they sort through the data they have collected with Mr. Fisher. They use this data to make Webpage reports as well as other exhibitions.

What exactly is student achievement in Mr. Fisher's middle school classroom? In brief, it involves both product and process, and achievement is assessed both individually and collaboratively. A key component of both the product and the process in this "new literacies" classroom is that the students need to be conversant in multiple forms of representation—they must collect and process a certain amount of information, including nonprint material such as photographs, video footage, and phone interview data. Also, students need to be able to think and talk about what they have done. The thinking and talking about the work is as much an expected achievement as is the product of the work.

Mr. Fisher echoes the thoughts of many new literacies teachers in that he believes there exists "official" achievement and "unofficial" achievement for his students. Some unofficial literacies are left out of the dialogue when we are talking about student achievement and remain hidden, missing, unassessed.

Kist 2003

How does authentic assessment complement standardized testing?

"Achievement is a tricky thing to me as it covers a lot of ground," said Clarence Fisher.

"There is the 'official' version of achievement which includes the students 'mastering' to the greatest degree possible the curriculum outcomes which have been mandated by the province I teach in. To me, this version is narrow and constrained and seems to be focused on very few things—academic knowledge, almost as a door to sort kids out, not to help them achieve more. On the other hand, achievement to me personally means having the kids work on an expanded set of skills which are useful to them now and hopefully as they grow into citizens of a 21st century, technologically-advanced nation."

A sign in Fisher's classroom states, "School is not about doing—it is about thinking and learning." "This is what achievement means to me," Fisher says. "It is about students pursuing a learning agenda that grows out of what we are required to do by the province, but which evolves as we examine the issue as a class to have some personal meaning."

Kist 2003

What about the current emphasis on comparing students with each other?

Pam Bauman teaches at Lafayette Elementary School in rural Medina, Ohio. Her classroom is infused with multiple forms of representation as students listen to music, examine newspaper advertisements, draw, design "quilts," work in various software, and, of course, read. Thinking about student achievement Bauman says:

Every school district feels the pressure to improve test scores as evidence of achievement. ... I can embrace high expectations for each child but resist the notion that if I teach harder, the students will learn faster. ... I believe there are developmental stages through which each child will pass at his or her own pace, and that is as it should be. The children learn on different schedules and in so many different ways—through song, movement, art, chatting with others—all of them valid. It is my charge to create those opportunities for learning that engage each child. It is my job to meet each student and take each as far as I can. To that end, I believe students achieve most when they are in a stimulating, joyful environment that encourages discovery and risk-taking. As their teacher, I want them to enjoy the "journey." Student achievement is evidenced by examples of their work over time in portfolios. [I look for evidence of] students who have honed social skills and students who have resources for solving problems. I have succeeded as their teacher if I have helped to mold students who can think, who have strategies for finding answers, and who are good friends and citizens.

Kist 2003

Indeed, authentic assessment provides students with the opportunity to develop 21st century skills of collaboration. Fisher's class also works on international collaborative projects; this year his students are collaborating with a class in the Netherlands on a project studying lifestyles and sustainable industries in both Manitoba and the Netherlands. The students are utilizing software called Knowledge Forum that Fisher describes as "a database with scaffolds. Students input data as they do research and these notes become searchable. [The software] has opened up our space—kids can input data and read comments from home or anywhere."

Kist 2003

Why is it important for students to be engaged in evaluating their own work?

Deeper thinking and higher level questions come from students working authentically. As they solve problems in the process of fine-tuning their product, performance, or portfolios; as they receive feedback from peers, experts, and teachers and then as they collect feedback at the work's completion, they have a unique opportunity to learn by making applications.

Lee Rother teaches in an alternative setting housed in Lake of Two Mountains High School, a school for grades 7–11 in suburban Montreal. [One day] his "at risk" students were chanting in unison the shot numbers as they examined a storyboard (with numbered scenes) for the crop duster sequence in Hitchcock's North by Northwest. As the scene played silently, students closely matched the storyboard with what was actually put on the screen. As each edit occurred, students shouted out in unison the corresponding scene number. Meanwhile, two students were in the back of the room working to create an animated graphic design using Flash animation software. Another student worked nearby editing a video on a desktop computer. Dr. Rother had brought in some raw footage from a family wedding, and the assignment was to weave the footage together into a coherent story using titles, graphics, and editing techniques. As I watched over his shoulder, the student had set up his first title which read, "Once upon a time, there was a beautiful maiden." As much as this may look like a video production class, it is not. It is an English class.

How does Rother conceptualize achievement in such a learning environment? When asked, like Fisher, he compared and contrasted the official sanctioned achievement with the unofficial achievement. "Really there are two ways to answer you; one is according to schooling's definition (i.e., marks, credits, and graduation). The other is my way." Rother goes on to say that the official signposts of student achievement in his school include having students complete coursework in which they have fallen behind and being able to go on to some kind of further education.

"My (own) definition of student achievement is first, completing two years in my program (especially suffering under my teaching); completing two to four work study sessions; developing self-confidence; opening up in terms of communication skills; and, emotionally, desiring to learn and continue learning in and out of school, and no longer (being) resistant to writing and reading print."

In Rother's classroom, there is much explicit discussion of all of the tools of communication and how those tools can be used. One of Rother's students,

Steve, described how he had learned to "read" a movie:

> "Basically, it's taking down mental notes on everything that does happen in a movie—foreshadowing, for instance, like small things, like why things happen in a movie, and for what reason exactly—the background, the lighting, the mood, the settings. There's a lot of things that take place. ... You just look at the movie differently. You realize it more." Interestingly, Steve comments on his ability to draw on these critical "reading" skills when he interacts with print: "When you read a book, you basically see it as if you are watching a movie, but you're reading. We learned to read a movie, so now, when you read a book, it's like, basically reading the movie."

Kist 2003

What are the links between the standards and the assessed outcomes of the learning?

Standards are necessary to guide task design. Standards of a broad nature are consistent with authentic assessment's emphasis on complex, integrative authentic tasks that typically span more than one class period, more than one topic and sometimes even more than one discipline.

Thus, good authentic assessment development begins with the standards that capture what we most value and want our students to learn. State and national efforts at standards-writing have typically focused on the content of the disciplines. Critical thinking skills, problem solving abilities, collaborative skills and personal development are other highly valued skills that are often covered in process standards, but are more difficult to test using traditional tests.

You can start by asking students to demonstrate what the standard asks of students (for example, solving math problems involving fractions). Or, you can ask yourself: Where would they use these skills in the real world? (follow recipes, order or prepare pizzas, measure and plan the painting or carpeting of a room, etc.)

Mueller, 2011

How do I decide what types of assessment tools and techniques to use?

Many factors play a part in this decision, including

- your teaching experience
- your knowledge and comfort with authentic assessment techniques
- the ages and backgrounds of your students
- the support of your team members and administrators

For each tool/technique/strategy, you need to answer

- What is its purpose?
- Is it student-focused, instructionally supportive, and outcome-based?
- What does the information tell you about each student's development? Will it be an effective diagnostic tool for students' knowledge and skills?
- How will this information help you make curricular/instructional decisions about the student? How will it help you address learning gaps? Will it help to motivate students to learn more?
- How often will you collect the information?
- Where will you store the information?

Hill and Ruptic, 1994; Greenstein, 2010

Discussion Prompts

1. Which of these items best reinforce and support your classroom or schooling experiences? Least reinforce and support your classroom or schooling experiences?

2. What issues discussed here do you feel are the most challenging? The most interesting? The most universal?

References

Erb, T. (2003). Using *Middle School Journal* for professional development, *Middle School Journal, 35*(1), 6.

French, D. (2003). A new vision of authentic assessment to overcome the flaws in high-stakes testing. *Middle School Journal, 35*(1), 14-23.

Greenstein, L. (2010). What teachers really need to know about formative assessment. Retrieved from *http://www.ascd.org/publications/books/110017/chapters/A-Study-Guide-for-What-Teachers-Really-Need-to-Know-About-Formative-Assessment*

Guskey, T. (Ed.). (1996). *Communicating student learning. 1996 ASCD year book.* Alexandria, VA: Association for Supervision and Curriculum Development.

Hill, B., & Ruptic, C. (1994). *Practical aspects of authentic assessment: Putting the pieces together.* Norwood, MA: Christopher-Gordon.

Kist, W. (2003). Student achievement in new literacies for the 21st century. *Middle School Journal, 35*(1), 6-13.

Mueller, J. (2011). Authentic assessment toolbox. Retrieved from jfmueller.faculty.noctrl.edu/toolbox

Rothstein, R. (2000, September 13). How standardized tests drop the ball. *New York Times,* p. B11.

Literature Reading #2:
Formative and Summative Authentic Assessment

Adapted from Effective Classroom Assessment: Linking Assessment with Instruction by Catherine Garrison, Dennis Chandler, and Michael Ehringhaus (2009)

Background: Summative Assessment

In a balanced assessment system, both *summative* and *formative* assessments are an integral part of data gathering. Depend too much on one or the other, and the reality of student achievement in your classroom becomes unclear.

Summative assessments are given periodically to determine at particular points in time what students do and do not know. Standardized state assessments are one form of summative assessment. At the district and classroom level, summative assessments are generally used as part of the grading process. Examples of summative assessments are state assessments, district benchmark or interim assessments, end-of-unit or chapter tests, end-of-term or semester exams, and scores used for accountability (AYP) and student report card grades.

Think of summative assessment as a means to gauge, at a particular point in time, student learning relative to content standards. Although the information gleaned from this type of assessment is important, it can only help in evaluating certain aspects of the learning process. Because they are spread out and occur after instruction every few weeks, months, or once-a-year, summative assessments are tools to help evaluate the effectiveness of programs, school improvement goals, curriculum alignment, or student placement in specific programs. Summative assessments happen too far down the learning path to provide information at the classroom level and to make instructional adjustments and interventions *during* the learning process. It takes formative assessment to accomplish this.

Background: Formative Assessment

Formative assessment is part of the instructional process. When incorporated into classroom practice, it *provides information needed to adjust teaching and learning while they are happening.* In this sense, formative assessment informs both teachers and students about student understanding at a point when timely adjustments can be made. These adjustments help to ensure students achieve targeted standards-based learning goals within a set time frame. Although formative assessment strategies appear in a variety of formats, there are some distinct ways to distinguish them from summative assessments.

One distinction is to think of formative assessments as "practice." We do not hold students accountable in "grade book fashion" for skills and concepts they have just been introduced to or are learning. We must allow for practice. Formative assessment helps teachers determine next steps during the learning process as the instruction approaches the summative assessment of student learning. Formative assessments can include products (p. 20), performances (p. 18), as well as homework, practice tests, first and second drafts, or personal communication strategies used by the teacher to collect information about student progress.

Chappuis and Stiggins (2008) state that

> By intentionally planning for more practice, we de-emphasize the competitive nature of school and give students a chance to grow with feedback, risk-free. Then, at some point, it is game day, when the teacher must make a judgment about the learning that has taken place. Leading up to that, teachers can review their assessment plan and ask:
>
> - Have all students been given sufficient practice with the right content at the right level of difficulty? Are they ready to succeed on the summative assessment?
>
> - Have I kept track of student progress by individual learning targets to know that they are ready?
>
> - Have the observations and results from practice been reviewed and fed back into the teaching and learning process?
>
> - Is there existing evidence of how well students have mastered the content that should "count?" Should any formative results contribute to the final grade? (p. 3)

Another distinction that underpins formative assessment is student involvement. Students must be involved in the assessment process for formative assessment to be fully effective. Students need to be involved both as assessors of their own learning and as resources to other students. Teachers can use authentic assessments to engage students. Research shows that the involvement in and ownership of their work increases students' motivation to learn.

Chappuis and Stiggins say further

> Students can be involved in their own assessment by doing the following:

> - Identifying the attributes of good performance by using a rubric to analyze strong and weak anonymous work samples
>
> - Learning and using strategies to self-assess
>
> - Partnering with their teachers to set goals on what comes next in their learning based on current results
>
> - Generating their own practice tests or test items using their understanding of the learning targets and working with each other to prepare and deepen their understanding
>
> - Working with clearly communicated learning goals to keep track of their success and communicating that success to others, as in student-led conferences
>
> We want to make learning targets clear to students, give them feedback throughout their learning to help improve their performance, teach them how to generate their own feedback through self-assessment, and show them how to use the feedback and the evidence of their own progress to manage and adjust their own learning. (p. 4)

This does not mean the absence of teacher involvement. To the contrary, teachers are critical in identifying learning goals, setting clear criteria for success, and designing assessment tasks that provide evidence of student learning.

Descriptive feedback

One of the key components of engaging students in the assessment of their own learning is providing them with descriptive feedback as they learn. In fact, research shows descriptive feedback to be the most significant instructional strategy to move students forward in their learning. Descriptive feedback provides students with an understanding of what they are doing well, links to classroom learning, and gives specific input on how to reach the next step in the learning progression. In other words, descriptive feedback not a grade, a sticker, or "good job!" A significant body of research indicates that such limited feedback does not lead to improved student learning.

The important next step is to figure out what to do with the information gathered. How will it be used to inform instruction? How will it be shared with students to further engage, motivate, and challenge them? It's not teachers just collecting information/data on student learning; it's what they do with the information they collect. Some of the instructional strategies that can be used formatively include the following:

Criteria and goal setting with students engages them in the learning process by creating clear expectations. In order to be successful, students need to understand and know the learning target/goal and the criteria for reaching it. Establishing and defining quality work together and determining what should be included in criteria for success are examples of this strategy. See pages 83–86. Have students contribute or create rubrics for their assessments to focus them on meeting the standards. Using student work, classroom tests, or exemplars of what is expected helps students understand where they are, where they need to be, and an effective process for getting there.

Observations go beyond walking around the room to see if students are on task or need clarification. Observations assist teachers in gathering evidence of student learning to inform instructional planning. This evidence can be recorded and used as feedback for students about their learning or as anecdotal data shared with them during conferences.

Questioning strategies provide opportunities for deeper thinking and provide teachers with significant insight into the degree and depth of understanding. Questions of this nature engage students in classroom dialogue that both uncovers and expands learning. Authentic assessment tasks provide prime opportunities for helping students ask better questions.

Self and peer assessment allow students to reflect while engaged in metacognitive thinking and be involved in their learning. When students have been involved in criteria and goal setting, self-evaluation is a logical step in the learning process. With peer evaluation, students see each other as resources for understanding and checking for quality work against previously established criteria.

Student record keeping, the process of keeping ongoing records of their work, not only engages students, it also helps them, beyond a "grade" to see where they started and the progress they are making toward a learning goal. From it they learn to evaluate information sources and articulate their learning for others, a real-world skill.

Summary To better understand student learning, teachers need to consider information about the products and performances students create and tests they take, observational notes, and reflections on the communication that occurs between teacher and student or among students. When a comprehensive assessment program at the classroom level balances formative and summative student learning/achievement information, a clear picture emerges of where a student is relative to learning targets and standards. Students should be able to articulate this shared information about their own learning. When this happens, student-led conferences, a formative assessment strategy, are valid. The more we know about individual students as they engage in the learning process, the better we can adjust the instruction to ensure that all students continue to achieve by moving forward in their learning.

References

Chappuis, S., & Stiggins, R. (2008). Finding Balance: Assessment in the middle school classroom. *Middle Ground, 12*(2), 1–4.

Garrison, C., Chandler, D., & Ehringhuas, M. (2009). *Effective classroom assessment: Linking assessment with instruction.* Westerville, OH: National Middle School Association; Measured Progress.

Questions

1. Record your assessment practices over a period of time; include the type (pre-assessment, formative, summative), the specific strategy used, a description of how you applied the strategy, the standards addressed, and how the resulting information was used.

2. What are the characteristics of formative assessment?

3. How are authentic assessment tasks suited as formative assessments?

4. How are students involved in their own assessments?

5. What are the benefits of peer assessments and students serving as resources for each other?

6. How do you use descriptive feedback to engage students and move them forward in their learning?

7. What assessment accommodations or adaptations do you use for various students?

8. Review your record of assessment practices (#1 above):

a. Is one assessment type more prevalent than the others?

b. What are commonalities and differences with other on your team/in your learning community?

c. Brainstorm ways to include assessments that are not currently evident or are used infrequently. How might you use the information from these assessments to inform your instruction?

Glossary of Assessment Terms

alternative assessment: Assessment that differs from the multiple-choice, timed, "one-shot" approaches that characterize most standardized and some classroom assessments.

analytic rubric: Scoring rubric designed to indicate the level of performance of a student's work on two or more separate elements of quality.

anchor: Representative product or performance used to illustrate each point on a scoring scale. Anchors for the highest score point are sometimes referred to as exemplars.

assessment: A broad term referring to the process of gathering and synthesizing information to help understand and describe.

authentic assessment: Measurement of student performance based on tasks that are relevant and useful in real life. It presents tasks that are worthwhile, significant, and meaningful, in short, "authentic."

authentic learning: "Commonly refers to learning about and testing real life situations, that is, the kinds of problems faced by adult citizens and consumers or professionals in the field," states Grant Wiggins. Authentic learning situations require teamwork, problem-solving skills, and the ability to organize and prioritize the tasks needed to complete the project.

benchmark: A standard for judging a performance. Schools develop benchmarks to tell what students should know by a particular stage of their schooling; for example, *By the end of sixth grade, students should be able to locate major cities and other geographical features on each of the continents.*

concept map: A graph or drawing consisting of nodes that represent concepts or key terms connected by labeled lines. The lines denote a relationship between a pair of concepts, and the label on each line describes the relationship between the two concepts.

criteria: Guidelines, rules, or principles by which student responses, products, or performances are evaluated.

evaluation: Involves making a judgment regarding quality, value, or worth, based upon criteria.

fairness: Refers to giving all students an equal chance to show what they know and can do. Fairness is compromised when teachers assess something that hasn't been taught or use assessment methods that are incongruent with instruction.

formative assessment: Refers to ongoing, diagnostic assessment that provides information to help teachers adjust instruction and improve student performance.

generalizability: The extent to which the performances sampled by a set of assessment activities are representative of the broader domain being assessed.

higher-order thinking skill: Complex reasoning skill that asks students to go beyond the basic skill of memorizing information by developing their ability to process information and apply it to a variety of situations through use of taxonomies such as those developed by Bloom and Williams.

holistic rubric: Scoring rubric intended to provide an overall impression of the elements of quality and levels of performance in a student's work.

learner outcome: Clearly defined content knowledge or skill related to the topic being studied that students are expected to demonstrate through completion of authentic tasks.

multiple validation: A variety of authentic tasks provide performance indicators regarding achievement of program (content) outcomes.

naturalistic observation: Sometimes called *kidwatching*. Consists of teachers observing individuals and groups as teachers and students go about their daily work. Teachers observe individual and group behaviors related to academic tasks, work habits, thinking processes, and other activities that influence student performance. The interaction among students in work situations and social settings provides an important focus for naturalistic observation.

pedagogy: The art of teaching, especially conscious use of particular instructional methods.

performance assessment: Teachers or audiences directly observe students applying desired skills and knowledge in oral presentations, demonstrations, or debates.

performance task: Activity, exercise, or problem requiring students to show what they can do. Some performance tasks are designed to have students demonstrate their understanding by applying their knowledge to particular situations. The process involves the use of higher-order thinking skills. Performance tasks may be used primarily for assessment at the end of a period of instruction but are frequently used for learning as well as assessment.

portfolio: A file or folder containing a variety of information that documents a student's experiences and accomplishments over time. The portfolio can contain summary descriptions of accomplishments, official records, alternative test formats, diary or journal entries, work samples, product or performance artifacts, and completed assignments.

probe: Question asked by the teacher to elicit responses related to a specific content topic, skill, or thinking process.

product assessment: Tangible indicator of the application of knowledge and skills through written product (essay, lab report, research paper), visual product (model, display, movie), or aural product (oral presentation, aural tape).

proficiency: Having or demonstrating a high degree of knowledge or skill in a particular area.

profile: Unlike a portfolio, a profile is not created by an individual student and does not contain actual samples of work. Rather, a profile is a form that teachers, students, and sometimes parents fill out with ratings and summary judgments or descriptions of achievement.

reflective journal: Notebook or digital format in which students write about and respond to what they have learned, including questions, comments, and notes of what they don't understand.

reliability: Determines the dependability and consistency of assessment results.

scoring rubric: A fixed measurement scale of four to six points and sets of criteria that describe the characteristics for each score point.

selected-response item: A testing format that presents students with a question, problem, or statement followed by a set of alternative responses. Students make a selection from among the given alternatives rather than generate their own responses. This format allows teachers to assess students' knowledge of factual information, concepts and principles, and the application of basic skills efficiently and objectively.

summative assessment: Refers to any culminating assessment that provides a summary report on the degree of knowledge or proficiency attained at the conclusion of a unit, course, or program of study.

testing: One type of assessment that has a set of questions or situations designed to elicit responses that permit an inference about what a student knows or can do. Tests most often utilize a paper-and-pencil format, occur within established time limits, restrict access to resources, and yield a limited range of acceptable responses.

validity: Determines whether an assessment measures what it was intended to measure.

Bibliography

Books and Journals

Armstrong, T. (2009). *Multiple intelligences in the classroom* (3rd ed.). Alexandria, VA: Association for Supervision and Curriculum Development.

Berckemeyer, J., & Kinney, P. (2005). *The what, why, and how of student-led conferences.* Westerville, OH: National Middle School Association.

Elliott, L. (2011). *Teach like a techie: 20 tools for reaching the digital generation.* Peterborough, NH.

Garrison, C., Chandler, D., & Ehringhaus, M. (2009). *Effective classroom assessment: Linking assessment with instruction.* Westerville, OH: National Middle School Association; Measured Progress.

Johnson, S. (2011). *Digital tools for teaching: 30 E-tools for collaborating, creating, and publishing across the curriculum.* Gainesville, FL: Maupin House.

Kaye, C. B. (2004). *The complete guide to service learning.* Minneapolis, MN: Free Spirit.

Kist, W. (2003). Student achievement in new literacies for the 21st century. *Middle School Journal, 35*(1), 6–13.

Lounsbury, J. H., & Schurr, S. L. (2003). *Assessing student progress: Moving from grades to portfolios.* Westerville, OH: National Middle School Association.

Mueller, J. (2011). Authentic assessment toolbox. Retrieved from www.jfmueller.faculty.noctrl.edu/toolbox

Palmer, E. (2011). *Well spoken: Teaching speaking to all students.* Portland, ME: Stenhouse.

Spencer, J. (2008). *Everyone's invited: Interactive strategies that engage young adolescents.* Westerville, OH: National Middle School Association.

Spencer, J. (2010). *Teaming rocks: Collaborate in powerful ways to ensure student success.* Westerville, OH: National Middle School Association.

Smith, G., & Throne, S. (2009). *Differentiating instruction with technology in middle school classrooms.* Eugene, OR; Washington, DC: International Society for Technology in Education.

Internet Resources

Virtual field trips   *http://www.tramline.com*

Roleplaying   http://serc.carleton.edu/introgeo/roleplaying

Rubrics   *http:// rubistar.4teachers.org*

Student presentation rubric   *http://www.ncsu.edu/midlink/rub.pres.html*

Webquests   *http://webquest.org/index.php*

Blogs   *http://wordpress.org*

Wikis   *http://PBWorks.com*

Service learning   *www.servicelearning.org*

Middle school debate program   *www.middleschooldebate.com*

Connecting with experts   *www.edutopia.org/connecting-experts-real-world*

American Association of School Librarians' Best Websites for Teaching and Learning
http://www.ala.org/ala/mgrps/divs/aasl/guidelinesandstandards/bestlist/bestwebsitesop25

Teaching students to evaluate a website

- Literacy Resources   *http://novemberlearning.com/Resources/Information*
- UC Berkeley Library   *www.lib.berkeley.edu/Help/guides.html*
- Internet Use   *http://school.discoveryeducation.com/schrockguide*
  Click on Internet Information in the menu under Subject Access.

Free tools including "Choose the Best Search" to find directions for using search engines and their features for efficient searching   *www.noodletools.com*